The Charity First series aims to provide practical and straightforward guidance on the challenges confronting charity operations today, with fundraising in the spotlight. Its individual subjects range from those concentrating on the UK and Ireland to non-profit issues in the EU and other jurisdictions, from traditional to digital fundraising and from basic help for those just entering the third sector to specialist areas for the more experienced.

For further information and orders see www.charityfirstseries.org

EFFECTIVE MEDIA RELATIONS FOR CHARITIES

What journalists want and how to deliver it

Becky Slack

First published in Great Britain 2016 by
Social Partnership Marketing LLP
38 Leconfield Road, London N5 2SN

A CIP catalogue record for this book is available from the British Library.

ISBN: 978-1-908595-35-5

Printed in Great Britain by CPI Group (UK) Ltd, Croydon, CR0 4YY.

Effective Media Relations for Charities is also available in electronic format from www.charityfirstseries.org

For dad. The best storyteller I know.

Welcome from charitycomms

UK charities play a vital role in our society. With an annual spend of nearly £40bn, the sector provides a vast range of activities and services which, in the most general sense, all aim to improve the wellbeing of society. However, for a number of reasons, the sector as a whole is not always well understood by the public, nor always applauded for its work or its methods.

For individual charities – often reliant on voluntary contributions for their very survival – public perceptions of their value are especially important: every charity needs to able clearly to communicate how it's pursuing its mission and why it uses the methods it does. Indeed, in many cases, effective communications is itself a crucial part of the charity's mission.

As an extension of the general communication strategy, every charity should also have a clear media strategy – this will focus, on the one hand, on deciding what key messages are to be communicated to which audiences and, on the other, on understanding the roles of media professionals – and making them your friends.

I hope this book helps you develop such a strategy. It should give you a better understanding of how to make the case for media work; of what journalists want from charities; and of how you can make the most of your resources, however limited, to deliver it.

Vicky Browning, director, CharityComms

CONTENTS

INTRODUCTION

Charities' relationship with the media

As I write this guide, the charity sector is reeling from a seemingly unprecedented amount of negative media coverage. From fundraising techniques to salaries, many questions have been raised about the way in which charitable organisations operate. While some claim that the media are specifically targeting charities in a bid to weaken them, others believe the negative coverage is the consequence of years of failure to explain the realities of running a charity in a modern world. Either way, charities have been shown to be ill-prepared to cope when coverage turns sour.

Running alongside this is the sense that charities do not get the positive coverage they need and deserve, despite the sector containing a wealth of knowledge, experience and insight into the world's most pressing social challenges. Indeed, of the 167,000 charities currently registered in the UK, very few are recognised as household names.

Of course, there are some charity PR teams that work very effectively with the media, delivering great content in a way that meets both parties' needs – and we will meet some of these throughout this guide. However, for every charity PR that works well with journalists there are countless others that do not. My own experiences of working with charities, and those of my journalist colleagues, show that there are many ways in which charity PR and media relations could be improved. For instance, many charities: lack understanding as to what makes a good news story; are unable to provide strong, interesting and relevant case studies and; operate within slow and bureaucratic internal processes that result in missed deadlines. Most frustratingly of all, when the going gets tough, many have a tendency to stick their heads in the sand and hope it will all just go away (it won't).

None of these issues are insurmountable. With the right training and resources, many more charities can enjoy fruitful relationships with the media.

By helping charities to navigate through the complex media maze, this guide aims to contribute to addressing this issue, albeit in a small way.

I hope you enjoy the read.

Becky Slack, managing director, Slack Communications.
See About the Author (p112).

A note before you start reading:

The 'media' can mean many things to many people. As with 'charity' it is not one homogeneous group of journalists and outlets. It includes newspapers, television channels, individual radio programmes, blogs, online magazines and other digital sources – the size, scope and objectives of which vary enormously.

For the purposes of this guide, I use the term 'media' to mean those individuals who are tasked with reporting on what is happening in the world, be it via print, broadcast or online – unless explicitly stated otherwise.

It does not include 'social media' – as in Twitter, Facebook, LinkedIn and other digital channels that allow two-way interaction. Content can be posted on these channels by anyone with an internet connection. This content then can be commented on and shared by others. While these channels can be a good source of news stories and case studies, they are not the sole preserve of journalists and for that reason when this guide refers to 'media' it does not mean 'social media'. For more on social media, see Chapter 9 or see the blogs and guides available at www.charitycomms.org.uk.

You will also be introduced to Amber Valley Angels. This is a fictional charity that is used throughout the guide to help illustrate activities and provide context.

Media strategy: the key elements

When time, money and resources are tight, it's important you understand what you want to achieve with your PR activities and why. Being strategic is vital as this will enable you to present a consistent message that is heard by the right people at the right time.

Working through the strategic pillars below before embarking on media activity will help you and your organisation decide what you want to achieve and why. It can also help remove duplication of effort, enable resources to be directed precisely where they are needed, and avoid wasting time and money.

The strategic pillars are:

1. Objectives

What do you want to achieve and why? Do you want to raise awareness? Strengthen your reputation within a key area? Promote a fundraising campaign or petition? What does PR success look like to you and your organisation?

2. Target audience

Who do you want to talk to and why? As we will discuss in Chapter 2, there is no such thing as the general public. Be specific about who it is you want to engage with and what their information needs are, and then target your PR activities accordingly.

3. Tone of voice

What kind of personality do you want to convey? Are you fun and energetic? Authoritative and serious? The impression you want to create among your target audience will help determine the type of media outlet you want to work with, what you want to say to them and how you say it.

4. Key messages

What do you want people to think, feel or do? Your key messages will help explain your organisation and what it does, why this is important and the difference you make. See Chapter 3.

5. Content

Central to the success of your PR activity will be the quality of the stories you have to offer journalists. What case studies do you have? Do you have access to data that will help evidence your opinion or your work? See Chapter 4.

6. Media training

Knowing what you want to say is one thing. Having a spokesperson who can communicate this clearly and concisely, particularly under times of pressure, is another. Media training can help iron out any creases. See Chapter 7.

7.Crisis comms
Preparation is key if a crisis is to be averted or minimised. Understanding your strengths and weaknesses, and having a plan as to what to do if it all goes wrong, are essential to protecting your reputation. See Chapter 8.

8. Managing expectations
While you may understand the opportunities and challenges associated with PR, your senior management team and trustee board may not. Helping them to understand what is realistically achievable is important if you are to satisfy expectations (see page 101).

9. Monitoring and evaluation
Knowing what worked and what didn't will help you understand which areas of your strategy to change and to do more of, and will provide you with valuable insight to build the case for future investment. See Chapter 10.

1
OBJECTIVES: WHAT DO YOU WANT TO ACHIEVE AND WHY?

Why work with the media?

Page 3 and charity are unlikely bedfellows, but in 2014 a partnership with *The Sun* worked a treat for the breast cancer awareness charity, CoppaFeel! Its bold PR campaign, which used the newspaper's glamour models to encourage readers to check their breasts more regularly, got results – after eight months women were four times more likely to check their breasts than before and at least six women had cancer diagnosed as a result of the campaign[1].

Elsewhere, following the *Daily Mail* telephone fundraising exposé in July 2015, where it was alleged that overly aggressive tactics were being used to coerce old and vulnerable people into giving money, charities chose to put their use of this technique on hold, resulting in the loss of hundreds of jobs and many thousands of pounds to good causes. The government also held a review of self-regulation of fundraising and various charity sector leaders were hauled in front of the Public Administration and Constitutional Affairs Select Committee to explain their actions both of which resulted in new rules being introduced.

The media has reach and it has influence. This is why it offers such value to charities. Whether a charity wants to raise public awareness of an issue, highlight its successes, campaign for change, or build trust and confidence both in its own operations and those of the sector more widely, the media can be a very useful tool. It can also be dangerous and risky – as the *Daily Mail* example above demonstrates.

Tapping into the benefits and tackling the challenges is easier said than done, especially where cynical and time-pressed journalists are concerned. Successful media relations require a combination of skill, resources, good relationships – and a whole lot of luck.

Understanding how the media works

To secure the coverage they want and need, charities first need to understand journalism. As such our journey starts in the newsroom.

Charities are not the only organisations where resources are stretched.

[1] Coppafeel (https://coppafeel.org/)

The media has also experienced vast reductions in income, resulting in job losses and smaller budgets. Recognising the pressures and demands of the media will help you to understand the requests journalists make and the story ideas they will pick up.

There are more than 31,000 journalists working for more than 15,000 publishers and broadcasters, across more than 9,000 different titles, be these television news channels, national and regional newspapers, lifestyle magazines, or specialist hobby and trade publications. The value of the media is currently estimated to be £60bn each year to the British economy. Some £280m of this comes from magazines and periodicals, and £186m from newspapers. The remaining 99 per cent is from the plethora of broadcasters and online news and magazine websites. Each are influential in their own right: 75 per cent of people access news via television; 41 per cent of people access their news online via websites and mobile apps, including social media channels such as Twitter and Facebook[2], although this latter figure is growing all the time as smartphones and tablets become more prevalent.

The media is a white, male-dominated industry. Some 94 per cent of British journalists are white. Women are hugely under-represented; only 35 per cent of the *Observer*, *Daily Mail* and *Express* teams are female and just 25 per cent of the *Independent* team are women[3]. Britain has only ever had two female editors of a daily broadsheet newspaper – Rosie Boycott was editor of the *Independent* for three months in 1998 while more recently Katharine Viner was appointed as editor-in-chief of the *Guardian* after Alan Rusbridger stepped down. The tabloids have fared reasonably better thanks to Eve Pollard, Tina Weaver, Dawn Neesom and Rebecca Brooks, among others, but even so female editors are still a rare breed among the red tops.

It is a hugely competitive space. Most journalists are constantly on the hunt for the next big story, the front-page headline that their rival has missed or found too late, or the nugget of information that is going to turn their feature into one that will keep readers hooked.

The pressure that this competition creates is heightened all the more as a result of the large workload and tight deadlines most journalists are given. The internet has a lot to answer for here. Print sales have slumped[4]

---

2 PPA

3 New Statesman

4 ABC

by more than half a million over the past year, and publishers have yet to figure out how to make money online. As a result, this has led to a large number of redundancies. As this book goes to print, many journalists are discovering if they have lost their job as the *Independent* moves to a digital-only format. In 2014, the BBC alone made over 500 journalists redundant[5] while there have been numerous stories about Trinity Media journalists from around the country losing their jobs. At the same time, the 24/7 rolling news agenda demands a constant stream of content. Therefore, those journalists who are left have to do a whole lot more with far fewer resources.

While this situation can create challenges for those people attempting to pitch stories (see page 53), it can also create opportunities. The immediacy and volume of content that needs to be produced can be overwhelming, and journalists and editors frequently look to outsiders for help. This can provide openings for charity PRs – particularly those that can find a new angle on a current story, can quickly turn around a relevant blog or multimedia content, and have extensive social media networks around which they can also share content.

Journalists – who does what?

The number of full-time staff journalists that a media outlet employs varies enormously from one publication to the next. *Time* magazine, for example, has around 7,500 overall staff, several hundred of whom will be on the editorial team. But *Time* is not typical. It is an international news magazine with the huge budget and huge staff it needs to fulfil its aim of in-depth global news coverage. The emphasis is on writing and reporting with high-quality photography and graphics by way of illustration. The same applies to the BBC, which at the last count had around 800 journalists at its disposal – covering its 14 channels, nine radio stations and vast internet presence. In cases such as these, journalists will often have more stories at their disposal and more time to pull their stories together and can therefore be pickier over the content they choose to run, meaning charities will have to work much harder to secure coverage.

At the other end of the spectrum you will find magazines and broadcasters with much smaller teams to call upon. Most trade magazines, for example, will have an editorial team of one, two if they are lucky – which is responsible for the entire editorial output, both print and digital.

[5] BBC

They will decide on what content should run and will do all of the commissioning, editing and some writing. A freelance budget will rarely be available, therefore editors will be reliant upon contributors willing to write for free. This is where charity PRs can make themselves indispensable by providing a regular flow of suitable ideas and content.

More commonly, however, media outlets – whether they are print, digital or broadcast – will have a skeleton editorial staff, supplemented by freelancers. To find out how many staff a magazine has, check the mast-head or flannel panel (found within the magazine's pages) – these will reveal the writers, editors, etc. who work on it. In contrast, newspapers and broadcasters do not usually publish a staff list, although their rolling credits, websites and Wikipedia can be a useful source of information. Paid-for services such as Gorkana and PR Newswire also offer a database of contacts (more on this on page 63). All of this information will help identify who to pitch story ideas to.

A crucial point to remember is that the smaller the magazine, the more blurred the boundary between tasks performed by different members of staff. On some magazines, for example, everyone may take a turn at subbing, proofing, commissioning or writing. However, as a general rule of thumb...

Print publications

Editor/editor-in-chief: The most senior person on the team and the one with responsibility for its entire editorial output. Therefore, likely to be the busiest (and most stressed). They will not only decide upon the direction of the editorial but will often write and edit content and make sure it runs to time and to budget. They are also the public face of the publication so will be required to be at meetings, conferences and events – possibly even television and radio appearances. Only pitch to the editor if the magazine is small with few staff. For larger publications, your focus should be on the deputy, assistant, features and commissioning editors (see below for details).

Deputy editor: Often more hands-on than the editor, they will share some or all of the day to day tasks of the editor, with a key role in forward planning, commissioning and hiring.

Assistant editor/associate editor: Senior editors who in some cases will have responsibility for a particular section of the magazine.

Contributing editor: Probably freelance and will have similar duties to the deputy editor. This tends to be an honorary title that is given to VIP journalists and key influencers who mainly contribute ideas, articles and – importantly – contacts.

Features editor/commissioning editor: Responsible for coming up with story ideas and finding writers to produce them. In some instances they will also write content themselves. Charity PR people would do well to make friends with journalists with this title.

Sub-editor: Responsible for making sure the words fit the page, that house style (see Chapter 6) has been followed, and that all is accurate – grammatically, factually and legally. Will also write headlines and 'stand firsts' (introductory paragraphs).

News and feature writers: They do as their job title suggests. Should be the first port of call for news stories and feature ideas. They may have autonomy over which stories run or they may be responsible for pitching the ideas into the wider team. Either way, you should make friends with them.

Publisher: This person is responsible for the finance and strategic planning that support the publication of the magazine. Often will work across multiple titles at the same time.

Sales/Business development: The team to speak to about sponsorship and advertising opportunities.

Digital media

As above but with the additions of:

Online editor: Similar role as 'editor' above, but focusing purely on the content of the website, tablet edition and social media channels.

Community manager: They have responsibility for the management of the brand's online channels, driving and directing community conversation in areas such as lifestyle blogs, latest news articles and products to review, forum areas etc. They will manage content production and work with the more engaged community users on a one to one basis to ensure a steady flow of conversation that is on brand and on message.

Social producer: As well as being responsible for managing the Twitter and Facebook feeds for a brand, this person will also create content for publication with the intention of growing the follower base and levels of engagement.

Website co-ordinator: A media outlet may have multiple websites or large websites that contain a huge amount of information. The main focus of the website co-ordinator, therefore, is to develop the functionality of webpages and their content whilst working closely with a number of different internal teams including production and web development to ensure that the entire site is working as it should.

Broadcast media

Editor: The editor is responsible for the programme as a whole. They manage the budget, the staff, the talent, check for inaccuracies, influence content decisions. They are also to blame if things go wrong. This role is different to that of 'video editor' who is responsible for cutting different shots together to create a story.

Output editor: They work alongside the editor and are responsible for everything that happens on their watch, which may be anything from a day to a couple of hours. They'll choose the lead story and the running order, choose the guests and the way stories are treated. They will also brief reporters and presenters and give feedback after the programme.

Producer: Similar to an editor, a television producer is a person who oversees all aspects of a television programme. Some producers take more of an executive role, in that they conceive new programmes and pitch them to the television networks but upon acceptance they focus on business matters, such as budgets and contracts. Other producers are more involved with the day-to-day workings, participating in activities such as screenwriting, set design, casting, and directing.

Associate/assistant producers: As above but less senior and usually there to support the producer.

Planner: This person manages the forward planning diary and co-ordinates with the news team to ensure that stories are covered when they happen. Key tools in their armoury are their contacts book and their knowledge of what's happening and when.

Newsreader: This individual will present the news on either radio or television. They are usually journalists who have worked their way up through the ranks. Their job is as much about reading the news as it is about handling situations that go wrong, such as the autocue failing, a guest saying something they shouldn't or losing a live feed mid-way through an interview.

Journalist: Journalists collect, verify and analyse information about news and events and present that information in an accurate, impartial and balanced way, be it live or pre-recorded, on either TV or radio. Sometimes, if they work for large international broadcasters, they may find themselves having to conduct two or more simultaneous live reports around the world.

Director: The director is responsible for supervising the placement of cameras, lights, microphones and props. They will also give cues to presenters, actors and other players.

A day in the life of a tabloid journalist

To build a successful relationship with a journalist it's important to understand the priorities they are working to. **Ashitha Nagesh**, a news reporter for *Metro*, gives a flavour of her day:

It's become a bit of a cliché, but it holds true that as a journalist, no two days are the same. So I will give as full an account as I can of my day today. I was on a morning shift, so I woke up at 5am to get ready and get into the newsroom for 7am. Intermittently, as I'm getting ready I read the *BBC* website. On the way in, I read the paper edition of *The Times* and articles on the *Guardian* app on the tube, and grab a copy of the *Metro* to look at later.

The first thing I do when I get in is quickly scan the wires –

first I look at the Press Association day schedule, then Associated Press and Reuters, then all other agencies. Then, a very quick scan of a news aggregator (I use NewsNow) and the homepages of the *Sun* and *Mirror* websites to see what they're running. In the case of today, I've been working on a slightly longer-running (around a week) piece on a certain extremist who shall not be named. I had to chase up some experts in connection with that, so I sent off a bunch of emails and made a note to myself to call them later.

I was assigned the report on Cilla Black's funeral on my newslist, which I knew was starting at 1pm – so I made a note to start working on that around midday or 12.30pm and had a look for other stories.

My first story was about Donald Trump saying the Pope is an Islamic State target, and that capitalism "done properly" is the answer (somehow). He made the comments in an interview with Chris Cuomo on *CNN* so it was a relatively easy write-up. Later in the day I wrote an article about the murder of Anneli-Marie R in Meissen, Germany, which I wrote about a few days ago but I now had some follow-up information.

I also wrote up two court cases – the sentencing of an elderly paedophile who claimed God had "wiped his memory of the event" because he had forgiven him, and the tribunal hearing of a social worker who was dismissed after asking for her coffee to be made "n***** brown". On a typical day I will write between seven and nine stories, but today was an exception because the extremism article and coverage of Cilla Black's funeral both took significantly longer to do than your average story.

For Cilla's funeral, I started by writing a primer – around 12 paragraphs – which I set live in the *Metro* content management system with a couple of photos of people arriving and then built on as the service went on. By the end of the service this had grown to around 30 paragraphs, with a mixture of photos, videos and tweets that I'd been collecting as I wrote. I had a third cup of black coffee for lunch, finished work around 3pm and headed home to carry on chasing people about my extremist.

Chapter 1 in a nutshell

- To secure the coverage you want, you need to understand journalism. Only by recognising the pressures and demands of the media can you establish what a journalist wants and what they don't.

- The media is a competitive marketplace and has been subject to extensive budget and staff cuts. This is influencing the speed at which journalists work and the type of content and information they need.

- The immediacy and volume of content that needs to be produced can be overwhelming, and the media frequently looks to outsiders for help. This can provide openings for charity PRs – particularly those that can find a new angle on a current story, can quickly turn around a relevant blog, and have extensive social media networks around which they can share content.

- Different types of journalists have different demands. Understanding the nuances between print, digital and broadcast media should inform your PR strategy and influence your results.

2
AUDIENCES: WHO DO YOU WANT TO SPEAK TO AND WHY?

A charity PR has two main goals:

- To secure as much positive coverage as possible – particularly coverage that reaches key audiences.
- To keep negative stories out of the press (or manage negative stories if and when they appear) – particularly those that may influence the decisions and views of key audiences.

Each requires different tactics. That said, the first will help achieve the second. To accomplish these goals, an understanding of what journalists want and need is required.

What journalists want

According to Google's chairman, Eric Schmidt, every two days we as a species create as much information as we did from the dawn of civilisation up until 2003. It is mind boggling to think about and means it's almost impossible for one individual to research everything there is to know on a subject. Enter stage left, the journalist.

The role of a journalist is to investigate, collect and present information to their audience. It is their job to make sense of this plethora of data and present us with what we need to know, filtering out unnecessary content.

This information – and ideas about how best to filter and present it – are the raw materials with which they work, materials that are then crafted into shape for the use by or for the entertainment of the reader.

With this in mind, and given that journalists are required to deliver an increasing amount of content for the publications and broadcasters for which they work, it is relatively easy to establish what they want. At the most basic level, they want good ideas and useful, reliable information that will enable them to create stories that offer something new and interesting to their readers. They also want these to be delivered in the format they require and by the date and time they need it. There is nothing like a failure to follow a brief to irritate even the calmest and most patient of journalists.

Experiences from the receiving end

Understanding who you are pitching to is paramount. PRs frequently get this wrong, submitting wholly inappropriate requests to journalists.

The journalist **William Turvill** has kept a Twitter log of ridiculous PR requests he receives as part of his job as news editor of *Press Gazette*, the trade magazine for journalists. These provide an amusing example of what not to do.

"I've got a story for the Peckham Peculiar." *That's not us.* "How can I get hold of them?" *Google them and click on their website.*

"Would the Gazette cover our Year-Six theatre production?" *No.*

"How much to hire one of your photographers for the night?" *Err...* "This is the Gazette?? The Ealing Gazette?" *No, sorry.*

"We've got a photocall for Bernie Ecclestone tomorrow and I wondered who the best point of contact was?" *Not Press Gazette.*

"I need to get hold of [high-profile investigative reporter] urgently!" *He doesn't work here.* "Can I leave a message with you?"

"Put me through to the editor of Channel 4 – NOW!"

Hello? "Yeah, just put me through to the motoring section of The Daily Telegraph."

Hello, Press Gazette. "I'm so sorry, I've got the wrong telephone number." *Bless you, sir. Why can't they all be like you?*

You can follow William and *Press Gazette* – and learn more about journalism – at @wturvill and @pressgazette

Understanding the audience (and tone of voice)

At the very front of an editor or journalist's mind when working on content will be the needs of the reader or viewer. They will have very firm convictions about what is right for their channel and all content will be focused on serving the needs and interests of their audience. While their first function is to make money for the media owners, they also provide readers with a sense of community and identity.

As such, knowing the market, the media outlet's brand values, and the information needs of specific audience segments is vitally important to effective press relations. The most obvious example of this is the difference between tabloids and broadsheets. Typically, broadsheets tend to focus on in-depth coverage with a sober, authoritative tone of voice that reflects the intelligence of their readers, who tend to be fairly affluent and well educated. Conversely, tabloids tend to be more irreverent within their writing style, using slang and peppering hard news stories with adjectives, such as "shocking", "disgraceful" and "scandalous". This tone is reflected in the content, with a tabloid more likely to cover celebrity gossip and sensational crime stories than 'serious' news such as a major bill being debated in Parliament.

More subtle differences between media outlets might be their political allegiances (the *New Statesman* is a left-leaning politics and current affairs magazine while *The Spectator* is right-leaning, for example), the space that they can give stories (*Channel 4* news runs much longer investigative pieces than say *ITV* or *Sky News*), or the location of their readers (*Evening Standard* readers are based primarily in London or within the commuter belt). In the same vein, specialist trade magazines will focus very specifically on the niche business needs of their readers, be this the latest developments in social care or technological advances in engineering.

Nuances such as these will be a key determinant in pitching the type of content a journalist will be looking for. For example, there is no point pitching a story about a small local fundraising initiative to a national newspaper as this will have little interest to the majority of its readers. However, a local newspaper might be happy to run a story of this nature. Therefore, charity PRs should think about what is relevant for a particular channel and marry that to what they have to offer.

Local media

When thinking about PR, many people tend to assume that national media offers more value. However, this is not always the case. Local media can often offer more opportunities for charities, not least because their audiences are so focused. Equally, local media is often a more trusted and preferred source of information – a recent survey[6] for example found that

[6] YouGov and Havas PR, 2013

more people trust what they read in their local paper than what they read on Facebook, while as many as 67% of people rely on local papers for local news, with radio preferred by a further 35%.

The value of local media depends on your organisation. If how you are viewed by people who live and work where you do is important, and your overall communications strategy outlines a desire to strengthen relationships with local service users, donors or customers, then engaging with local media should certainly be one of your key tactics. Even if you're a national organisation, communicating with people on a local level can help them to identify with you more closely.

Local media covers newspapers, radio, television and digital media. As with all media, the local media landscape is changing, as newsrooms shrink and local papers and radio/TV stations close or merge, putting additional pressure on their journalists to source and create suitable content.

As for what type of content local journalists want – this is the same as what any other journalist wants. They want strong stories that offer something new and interesting to their readers. Where they differ from the national or trade press is that they are looking for stories that are specific to their local area. This might be a specific town or a whole county, so make sure you understand their reach before making a pitch.

What type of stories might local journalists be interested in?

- The difference a charity has made in the local area, particularly where there are local residents who have inspiring stories they are willing to share.
- Charity events, particularly those attended by local dignitaries, business and community leaders, sports figures and celebrities.
- Examples of how national and local government policies and practices are impacting upon people locally, particularly where there are case studies and/or data to back up any opinions.
- Key milestones, accomplishments and appointments for a locally based charity, for example, fundraising records broken, special anniversaries or a new high-profile chief executive.
- New fundraising and awareness raising campaigns that locally people are encouraged to participate in.
- Case studies, data and examples of services in relation to Awareness Days/Weeks/Months.

Digital media

One consequence of the spread of the internet and digital communications has been the introduction of digital media, such as social news websites. This in turn has seen the rise of a 'sharing' culture – where people repost and share content among their friends and online networks.

Reddit, for example, is the self-styled 'Front page of the internet' that offers an online message board format where users can share links and vote featured content up or down. The most popular stories take prominence on the site, while less popular stories sink to the bottom. Comments are actively encouraged as a means by which to add information, context and humour to the stories, and anyone can create a community (known as a subreddit) that focuses on particular themes. Reddit is a global phenomenon, with its seven billion pages being viewed by around 250 million unique visitors each month from more than 200 different countries[7].

Buzzfeed is another hugely popular site. Its shareable features focus on news, entertainment and a variety of extremely stylised lifestyle and listicle pieces (an article on the internet presented in the form of a numbered or bullet-pointed list), and it received more than 5.7 billion hits over the course of 2015[8]. Buzzfeed aims to tap into trending content and topics, and to get as many hits as possible on the site. Users are encouraged to rate (upvote) stories as well as to share them on social media sites, such as Facebook or Twitter, with the success of an article often being based on how many times it has been shared online.

Hits and shares are also a big deal for the media giant, the Huffington Post. This was one of the first big-hitting news aggregators and blogs to be populated with both original and non-original content – ie that from other websites and the newswires. The American site, that has both localised and international editions, comprises 63 sections offering news, satire and blogs focused on politics, business, entertainment, environment, technology and lifestyle, among other topics. Since its 2005 launch, the site has grown into a mecca for (unpaid) bloggers and is a leading example of savvy, modern content aggregation.

How to make friends with journalists

A journalist's contacts book is their most prized possession. It is these contacts that provide them with the heads-up on a potential story, background information and opinion. Therefore, finding your way into

[7] Reddit

[8] Quantcast

this contacts book, and becoming a go-to person should be a key goal. The more trusted and reliable you are as a source of information about your sector the more journalists will turn to you for contributions, be it in the form of interviews, written statements or articles and blogs.

While journalists working for mainstream national publications and broadcasters may be your priority, it is important not to forget about freelancers or journalists who work for specialist publications. Both are under-utilised by charities. Freelancers tend to have excellent networks and a finger on the pulse of multiple media outlets, while trade journalists are frequently asked by reporters who work for generalist titles to give quotes, background briefings or write comment pieces when a story breaks in their field of expertise – both of which could be advantageous to you if you play your cards right.

Journalists also move much more frequently between publications than they used to and someone who was once a junior on a trade magazine may ultimately become an influential commentator within the mainstream press. Hannah Fearn is a prime example of this – the former deputy editor of *Charity Times* magazine, she has held senior roles at the *Guardian* and the *Independent* wielding power over, news features, blogs and comment pieces that the newspapers have run both in print and online.

The relationships you build therefore have a huge part to play in your ability to place stories. But how do you go about doing this, particularly given journalists' intensely busy schedules? It is not something that you can do overnight. It requires concerted effort and planning.

Relationship-building techniques

My guidelines for establishing good working relationships with journalists are:

- Send them a briefing document containing information about your organisation, key spokespeople and the topics you can comment on.
- Send them useful, relevant and new information that meets the needs of their target audience and is presented in an appropriate format. Most journalists prefer email as the first point of contact.
- Know when NOT to pitch. Don't be the person calling a local

news station to pitch a story during the midst of a large fire at a nearby factory, or a national newsroom during a major terrorist siege. Breaking news stories can often consume the entire newsroom at which point no one will care about your organisation. Wait until things have calmed down.

- Be fast and reliable. Provide them with what they want, when they want it. One good interview or comment piece can turn into many more if the media know that you are responsive, efficient and can comfortably handle an interview.
- Make yourself available. News waits for no man or woman. Journalists need to know that they can call you at 7am or 11pm for comment and background information. Accommodating out of hours and urgent requests is essential if you're to become the go to person for interviews.
- Hang out where they hang out – conferences and events can be the best way to make that all-important first face-to-face contact.
- Invite them to meet you and your organisation. However, remember that journalists are busy and it has to be worth their while. The invite will only be accepted if you have something interesting to offer them that they couldn't receive over the phone or via email, be it a press conference, the chance to meet a VIP or to see your work in action.
- Become their ears on your industry. Feed them stories, provide on-and off-the record comment, and help them keep on top of the latest developments so they can break stories faster and better than their competition. This may include giving them exclusives (see page 56) and visual and audio elements, such as photos, infographics and video to accompany a story. Journalists are busy. The more you can package up for them to make their life easier the better, and the more likely your content will be accepted.
- Ask them what they want. If you secure an interview with a writer or reporter, it's a great opportunity to strike up a conversation about what else they may be interested in covering But do it at the right time. Wait until all logistics of your phone interview have been set up or after the TV filming has wrapped up. Let them know that you enjoyed working with them and then mention a few other story ideas to see if they would be interested.

- Don't forget about social media. Follow journalists on Twitter and Facebook, and try and find an appropriate but not obtrusive way to join in the conversation or provide them with answers to questions they may have raised.
- Thank them. Just as you'd thank a donor or volunteer for their support, you should also thank a journalist for giving you great coverage. Be gracious.

Establishing your own audience

As we will go into in more detail shortly, "charity doing good work" or "fundraiser raising money" doesn't necessarily constitute a good story. Sending blanket press releases out to anyone and everyone about how wonderful your organisation is just isn't going to cut it. Careful thought needs to be given to every single approach made – not just in terms of whether it meets the needs of the journalist but also those of your own organisation.

As previously mentioned, the target audience is a journalist's key consideration. The same applies to you. Who is it you want to reach and why? By understanding this, you can develop a press strategy that makes the most effective use of your (probably limited) resources.

The first thing to be aware of when determining your target audience is that there is no such thing as the general public. The information needs and wants of a teenager are very different to a pensioner, just as they are different for medical professionals and patients.

To establish who your audience might be, think about the change you are trying to bring about through your work and who it is who might be able to support you in that activity. What is it you want them to do, what is their role, how knowledgeable are they about the cause, are they time or money poor or rich? Are they looking for power and status, excitement and adventure, or an opportunity to enhance their skills and expertise?

All of these factors, along with demographics such as gender, age, ethnicity and geographical location, will influence your defined target audience. It is highly likely that you will have more than one audience, depending on what your communications objectives are.

It may seem easier not to bother establishing defined target audiences, but this is a false economy. It is impossible to speak to everyone equally and in the same manner. Failure to define target audiences will result in wasted time, energy and resources, and a diluting of messages that will ultimately not resonate with anyone.

For example, if you are only concerned with raising the profile of your charity among ministers or industry leaders then you needn't bother targeting women's lifestyle magazines. Equally, if you only operate within a particular region of the country then your priority is likely to be on building relationships with your local media rather than focusing on the national press.

Once you have defined your target audience, you then need to know as much about them as possible. What they think, what motivates them, which websites they visit, which newspapers they read and how active they are in social media, etc. At its most basic level, this means using common sense and some desk-based research. More thorough and therefore more accurate audience research would involve polls and surveys, focus groups and paid-for data from research companies such as YouGov, Ipsos Mori, Kantar and others.

Knowing your audience means that not only will you be targeting your efforts in the right place, but that you can create media campaigns that will be appealing. For example, when Cancer Research UK wanted to target young people with messages about skin cancer, it did so via a beauty campaign rather than a health campaign. By teaming up with models and skin clinics it highlighted how sunbathing can damage your skin and speed up the ageing process – the intention being to target younger people who were concerned with their appearance and unlikely to pay attention to messages purely focusing on the health impacts of sunbathing.

Establishing key audiences

Amber Valley Angels is a small (fictional) charity based in the Amber Valley region of Derbyshire. Its network of volunteers helps local older people live independent lives and remain in their own homes. They do this by delivering practical care, such as cooking, cleaning, dressing, shopping and transport services, and emotional support, such as a morning chat over a cup of tea, regular telephone calls and social outings.

Its PR activity is based on the following:

Objectives: Meet the needs of more local older people by securing more funding from donors, and more influence within the local authority

Strategy: Highlight the difference the charity makes and the value it offers the local community

Based on the above information, Amber Valley Angels was able to determine that its target audience comprised:

1. Decision-makers and budget holders at the local authority, particularly those people in the social services team who commission services from charities
2. Business leaders based in the Amber Valley region. This would have the dual purpose of building relationships with potential funders and promoting the benefits of volunteering and donating to their staff.
3. Parents and children of service users who live in the local area, letting them know services are available, encouraging them to donate and attend events.

Chapter 2 in a nutshell

- The role of a journalist is to investigate, collect and present information to their audience. It is their job to make sense of a plethora of data and present us with what we need to know, filtering out unnecessary content.
- Journalists want good ideas and useful, reliable information that will enable them to create stories that offer something new and interesting to their readers. They also want these to be delivered in the format they require and by the date and time they need it.
- The role of the charity media person or team is to secure as much positive coverage as possible and to keep negative stories out of the press (or manage negative stories if and when they appear).
- Who do you want to reach and why? Your target audiences should inform your PR strategy and focus your efforts on the right areas. However, be specific: remember there is no such thing as 'the general public'.
- To establish who your audience might be, think about the change you're trying to bring about through your work and who might be able to support you in that activity.

3
WHAT DO YOU WANT PEOPLE TO THINK, FEEL OR DO?

What is a key message?

At the centre of any good communications strategy, media facing or not, are your key messages. These outline exactly what you want to say, and what you want people to think, feel or do as a result. They will explain your reason for being, why your work/the cause/the issue in hand is important and the value you add to the situation. Any claims should always be backed up with evidence.

Key messages should also be tailored to your target audience so this means taking into account their own individual needs. Think about how expert they are, what their personal motivations might be and how relevant what you are saying is to their day-to-day lives. You may find that you need to modify them slightly depending on who it is you are talking to – in the case of cancer support, for example, a health care professional will have very different information needs to a member of the public who has recently been diagnosed with the disease, and therefore will probably require slightly different key messages and call to action.

If you do use different versions for different audiences, make sure they don't conflict or contradict each other. For example, media activity aimed at supporting a fundraising appeal may want to highlight how important and urgent the need is, whereas that aimed at highlighting how successful a charity's work is may want to show how the need has been addressed.

Most importantly, they need to be memorable and should avoid using jargon. You want your spokespeople to repeat these messages (or variations thereof) during any interviews they may give or articles they may write, so they need to be easy to understand, remember and repeat. That is not going to be achieved if they are long and peppered with complicated terms and technical language.

Defining your key messages

The most successful key messages are those that have been carefully thought through and considered against different scenarios. This could involve conducting a key messaging workshop with colleagues, particularly if your organisation delivers many different types of projects and services

The Charity First Series

The **Charity First Series** offers clear, reliable, accessible guidance for not-for-profit organisations and all who support them.

All titles are available as **PDF** downloads from *www.charityfirstseries.org*. See website for details of other formats available, and to join our mailing list for news of new titles.

Academy Schools – *From Conversion to Successful Operation*
Stephen Claus, Graeme Hughes, Tracey Johnson and Debra Morris

Beyond the Collection Plate – *Developing Church Income from Different Sources*
Steve Pierce
(also available as a paperback)

Data Protection for Fundraisers
Lawrence Simanowitz and Mairéad O'Reilly, Bates Wells & Braithwaite

Fundraising for Small Charities
James K Myers

Legacy Fundraising from Scratch
Simon George

Major Gift Fundraising
James K Myers

Organising and Operating a US Charity - *501 (c)(3)*
Kristin Konschnik and Jaime McLemore, Withers LLP

Prospect Research
Robin Jones and Rebecca Funnell

Raising Funds from Grant Makers
Simon George

Structuring Not-for-Profit Operations in the UK
Julian Smith and Elizabeth Jones, Farrer & Co

The Gift Aid Guide
Graham Elliott, Withers LLP

spm fundessentials

Social Partnership Marketing LLP
38 Leconfield Road, London N5 2SN - Tel: +44 (0)20 7704 6803

@Charity_1st

that make it difficult to establish one coherent story.

Most key messages can be developed by asking yourself what the issue is and why it's important now, what you are doing about it, and what you want other people to do.

A simple formula to remember this by is:

Need + Solution = Impact (+ call to action)

Amber Valley Angels' key messages

The charity's key messages focus on the value its volunteers bring to the local community:

1. There are 3,000 older people living in loneliness and isolation in the Amber Valley region.
2. People who are lonely and isolated are more likely to suffer serious accidents and experience depression.
3. Our volunteers support older people in Amber Valley by providing practical and emotional support, such as shopping and transport services, social outings and a shoulder to cry on.
4. By maintaining independent living and keeping people out of hospital and care homes, our services save Amber Valley local authority £100,000 each year; and create countless smiles and laughs (who can put a price on that?).
5. You can help us help others by donating now/volunteering working with us {delete as appropriate}.

Points 1 and 2 outline the situation and the need; point 3 provides the solution and point 4 the impact. Point 5 – the call to action – changes depending on the audience.

These key messages then form the blueprint for all of their communications, whether it's an interview with a journalist, a blog on their website or posts made across social media. Not all the key messages will be used at the same time, or need to be used verbatim, but they underpin everything Amber Valley Angels says to the media. This allows the charity to send out a clear and consistent message at all times, thus strengthening its reputation, demonstrating its authority and reinforcing the societal need within the minds of the public and other key influencers.

By having these key messages you can then establish what type of content to pitch to journalists. Using Amber Valley Angels as an example again, it can then look at securing coverage that reinforces this message.

This might include the following:

- Putting the chief executive forward for a live interview for local radio or television to comment on a new government report into the state of independent living today.
- Pitching a blog to the local authority website about the value of independent living services and their role in keeping older people out of hospital.
- Submitting a press release to local media about Amber Valley Angels' research into the impact of loneliness on wellbeing and mental health in older people.
- Pitching a feature to a lifestyle magazine focused on a case study of a local older person who has benefited from the charity's services, thus improving their health and wellbeing.
- Pitching a news story about an innovative new fundraising or social media campaign that focuses on volunteering and older people.
- Inviting a local journalist to shadow a volunteer for the day so they can write about the experiences.
- Hosting an event to celebrate a key milestone or anniversary and inviting along key business and council leaders and local press.

Chapter 3 in a nutshell

- At the centre of any good communications strategy, media facing or not, are your key messages. These outline exactly what you want to say, and what you want people to think, feel or do as a result.
- When developing key messages, ask yourself what is the issue, why is it important now, what is your organisation doing about it, and what do you want other people to do?
- Avoid jargon, keep key messages simple so they are easy to understand, remember and repeat.
- Repeat your key messages over and over again until you are sick of hearing them. Only then might other people have heard what you have to say.
- Once you have defined your target audience and key messages you can then decide which media you want to approach and the type of content you can provide them with.

4
YOUR CONTENT STRATEGY

The channel a story is being published in – whether television, radio, online or in print – will determine how it is presented. There are many different ways in which to present information. It is important to understand the differences between them so that you can pitch successfully and follow briefs accurately.

For example, online news has forced journalists to rethink the traditional storytelling process. Printed and broadcast news is quite a crude, linear format – what you see is what you get. There will be no new information until the next issue is printed or broadcast, be that within an hour, a week or longer, depending on the frequency of the programme or title. Online is different as it demands the constant updating of stories as and when new developments occur. A single news site can post dozens of different updates and stories every few minutes.

At the same time, online offers a different user journey – one where the audience can go from the home page to a related page from three weeks ago, to a totally different story, off to someone else's website and then back again, all within a few clicks. This is in contrast to print or broadcast which maintains more control over the order in which news is consumed.

This 'web' of content, which is driven by the audience, means journalists are required to think about other complementary elements, such as additional case studies, opinion pieces, multimedia content and links to other sites. The need for this extra content is driven further by social media and the desire to create content that goes viral. Listicles and infographics are particular favourites when it comes to social shares.

Core values

Many people think that journalists are only interested in negative or sensationalist stories. This is not the case. Journalists are only interested in good stories. Good stories are those that interest, surprise or shock people. And for stories to be accessible people have to be involved – what's commonly known as 'human interest'. People like to read/hear about other people. They like stories they can relate to or about issues they can talk about.

For instance, if an announcement is made in a trade magazine about a company going into administration it is likely to be presented in terms of job losses. If a new mobile phone has been launched, it is likely to be written about in terms of what it has to offer the user, be it time saved or better functionality to make life easier. If a charity hits the headlines, it is either about the difference it has made to someone's life, how much its chief executive earns or how irritating the public finds particular fundraising techniques.

Therefore, the best stories are those which have people at the centre. This does not always mean the story has to be negative or sensationalist.

Case studies

Given the need to provide stories about people, it makes sense to look first at case studies – that all-important ingredient for many types of content. Charity PRs must know how to provide these.

A case study tells a story through the eyes of the people involved. It might be the story of a beneficiary and how their life was improved by the work of the charity; it might be the story of a donor who is sharing their experiences of giving to the cause; or it might be the story of people who work and volunteer within the organisation. The important factor, whoever the subject, is that it paints a picture of an event or situation and, through the experiences of others, evokes an emotional response.

The provision of case studies is an area where charities often hit below the mark. My own experiences and those of my colleagues is that while many PRs recognise their importance, they are frequently unable to meet expectations.

One way to assess if the case study is strong enough, is to apply the 'So what?' test (see page 38).

Take the case of a young boy who has difficulty reading, and who is supported by a volunteer. This story becomes much more interesting if, for example, the young boy is from a broken home, has experienced abuse and has behavioural difficulties, the last of which have been addressed at the same time as his reading skills have improved. In other words, triumph over tragedy. Anything less than that and a journalist is unlikely to accept it.

Fail to provide any case study at all and the likelihood of your story running falls even further. Charities often hide behind the excuse that they need to protect the privacy of their people. Yet all too often this is unfounded. I have frequently worked with organisations that insist that they absolutely do not have anyone they can put forward for an interview due to the highly sensitive nature of their work. However, when pushed to ask a service user how they would actually feel about it, they often find they have misjudged the situation, and that beneficiaries and supporters are very willing to tell their stories.

Providing case studies in pre-written format will be suitable for some journalists but not for all. In the main, they will want to speak to the person/s involved themselves so they can draw out all the information they need for their article. This means the case study in question must be articulate enough to tell their story.

If it is the case that your beneficiaries do not want to be identified, speak to the journalist to see if they would accept an anonymous case study or will change the name of the individual. While this is not ideal – most journalists prefer all interviews to be 'on the record' (see page 74) and properly attributed – they are often willing to discuss it if it means they will secure an important story.

Case studies featuring vulnerable people

Charities working within very sensitive areas, such as those that involve death or traumatic incidents, need to be mindful of the emotional wellbeing of their case studies during interviews.

Journalists are not always the most sensitive of people, particularly when they are up against a deadline or need to secure a headline-grabbing article. They are likely to expect a case study to be available at short-notice, and to relive difficult moments from their life in intimate detail.

This is something **Rose Dixon**, chief executive of SAMM, the national UK charity that supports families bereaved by murder and manslaughter, takes into consideration when putting people forward for media interviews.

Journalists frequently come to her with requests for case studies of people who have lost relatives through murder. Not only can the interviews be conducted at short-notice or inconvenient times, but it can be very painful for them to access highly traumatic memories.

Rose tries to prepare them as much as possible beforehand, including warning them that what they say might be quoted in different places for many years to come – particularly around anniversaries of incidents – and often when they least expect it. Peer support via SAMM's network of volunteers is also on offer.

Domestic abuse charity SafeLives also has to be very careful about who it puts forward for case studies. It facilitates a support network within the charity for survivors and friends/family who have lost loved ones to domestic abuse. It has trained professionals in its team to support survivors throughout any media events or opportunities; it ensures there is always a SafeLives staff member at all journalist interviews and that all survivors know they have the opportunity before, during and after to withdraw from the story.

Names are changed when necessary and risk is assessed on a regular basis. SafeLives also believes that those brave enough to become case studies must have ownership over their own story, and therefore would not expect them to talk to SafeLives key messages, but instead tell their own story, on their own terms.

It can be useful to offer media training to people being put forward as case studies so they understand what is expected of them and to help them deliver a good interview that meets the journalist's needs. It may also serve you well to speak to the journalist beforehand so that they are fully aware of any emotional and physical issues and how you would prefer those were handled. While journalists can sometimes be insensitive they are not completely heartless, and they will also want to get the best possible interview from the person in question.

Even if the interview goes well, the journalist may decide not to use it – no matter how much time and energy you have contributed to the story. Don't expect them to contact you to let you know if and when the story is to be used. They will be too busy and have too many other more urgent priorities to address. It is your responsibility to follow up on the information you and your case study have provided.

CharityComms offers a free best practice guide to handling case studies – see Useful Resources on page 110.

News

What is news? The clue is in the title.

A frequent complaint from the journalists I speak to is that many organisations – not just charities – treat PR as a branch of their marketing department. Rather than thinking about what makes an interesting and relevant story for readers/viewers, they see news as an opportunity to promote their work, products, services and campaigns.

Promotional puff does not make a good news story, but it does work as a paid-for advertisement. Journalists have an insatiable desire to retain their independence and usually dislike having to produce content that could be mistaken for advertorial (content that has been paid for by a sponsor). Personal conscience aside, the credibility of a media outlet can also be damaged if readers suspect there is too close a liaison between a journalist and a corporate interest.

Journalists also tell me that many press releases they receive that supposedly contain news are uninteresting and irrelevant for their target audience. So the lesson here for any charity PR trying to pitch a story is to make sure that it is actually news – ie something that the journalist and their readers didn't already know.

How can you determine what a news story is?

Back in the 1960s, Johan Galtung and Mari Ruge, media researchers from Norway, analysed international news stories to find out what factors they had in common. The news values they developed off the back of this research still hold true today and provide a good starting point for any charity PR considering what type of story to pitch (see box below).

That said, don't forget that journalists and editors also draw heavily upon their own knowledge of their target audience, which stories have performed well in the past and what fits with the individual publishers' and broadcasters' own agenda, so getting to know individual reporters and writers can also help you to determine what angle to present.

Applying the 'So what?' test

A good rule of thumb to apply against any story is the 'So what?' test. Will anyone but you actually care about the story you're pitching? How does it add value to their lives? Why do they need to know this information? Does it tell them something they don't already know?

The simple fact of the matter is that most people are not desperate to hear about your organisation and the work it does, so simply telling them about what you do isn't going to cut it.

Your stories have to be interesting and relevant to your audience. They need to understand why the story matters and why they should spend their valuable time listening to or reading about this when they could be doing something else instead.

Telling a shareable story with mass-media appeal

Antony Nolan was able to turn a patient appeal into a global feel-good story by applying some creative thought to the campaign.

The #Shake4Mike campaign was focused on finding a stem cell donor for Mike, 29, who had been diagnosed with leukaemia. Working very closely with Mike's fiancée Kate, the challenge was to create a shareable campaign that would have mass media appeal encompassing traditional press, broadcast and social as well as maximise links in Mike's local community and beyond. The ultimate aim was to encourage more males aged between 16 and 30 to sign up to the Anthony Nolan register.

Mike, Kate and their friends came up with a concept this age group could relate to: #Shake4Mike, which encouraged people to register at anthonynolan.org, shake their face at cancer while taking a selfie, share the image and the Anthony Nolan URL on social media and nominate others to do the same. The severity of Mike's illness gave the team just two months to find a donor match.

Rather than focus solely on the need for a match, which wouldn't have been considered new or interesting to journalists, the focus of the campaign was romance, focusing on how the couple had just "60 days to save a love story".

In one month, the #Shake4Mike campaign achieved a combined circulation reach of 160.6 million. An organic celebrity following began to build including Stephen Fry, Coldplay and Gary Lineker, and coverage was secured across national and regional print, digital and broadcast media. Over 9,000 donors registered on the charity's website during the period of the campaign and Anthony Nolan found a donor for Mike weeks later.

Why was it successful? #Shake4Mike tells a story of a race against time and, above all, one woman's dedication to the man she loved. As a result, media interest in the story was phenomenal. National media particularly embraced the role social media played in this 'love story for modern times'.

To read the full case study, visit www.charitycomms.org.uk/articles/how-did-a-patient-appeal-become-a-global-feel-good-story

News values

"When a dog bites a man that is not news,
but when a man bites a dog that is news."
Attributed to Charles Anderson Dana (1819-1897), American journalist

Negativity: Bad news, such as that involving death, tragedy, bankruptcy, violence, damage, natural disasters, political upheaval or extreme weather.

Proximity: Audiences relate more to stories that are close to them geographically, or involve people from their country – for instance a plane crash where British people were among those killed.

Recentness: Journalists are competitive about breaking news – revealing stories as they happen. They want to be the ones that brought it to you first.

Currency: Stories that are already in the public eye but are deemed valuable and so run and run, even if nothing new really happens, such as a child abduction or the birth of a royal baby.

Continuity: Events that are likely to have continuing impact have a high news value as they will develop into an ongoing narrative that will encourage audiences to come back for further updates. Wars, elections and sports tournaments are good examples of this.

Uniqueness: "Dog Bites Man" is not a story. "Man bites dog" is. Any story that covers a unique or unusual event has news values.

Simplicity: Stories that are easy to explain (train accident kills 100 people) are often preferred over stories that are not (Libor rigging). When the story is complex, it is the journalist's role to present the information in a way that is easy to understand. That might be via an interview with an expert who has to explain what has happened in layman's terms.

Personality: Stories that centre around a particular person, especially if that person is well-known, as these can be presented from a 'human interest' angle (see page 45 for more on celebrities).

Predictability: Does the event match the expectations of a news organisation and its audience? If a news story conforms to the preconceived ideas of those covering it then it has value. For example, violence at a demonstration, horrific casualties in a terrorist attack.

The elite: Any story that covers an important, powerful nation, organisation or person has greater value than one that covers a less important one.

Exclusivity: If a newspaper or broadcaster is the first and only news outlet to be breaking a story then they will rate it highly. The Sunday papers are fond of this approach (see page 56).

Size: Size does matter. The bigger the impact, the more people affected, the more money or resources involved, the higher its value.

The lifecycle of news

There are two types of news stories: hard news, which is the basic reporting of something that has happened; and news analysis, which features people's (often the journalist's) opinions on what happened. In either case, they will have a lifecycle. There are opportunities for savvy charities to find opportunities to pitch to journalists throughout all the lifecycle stages.

These stages go something like this:

Stage 1: Preview
Some news, such as the staging of important political events or major sporting events can be previewed. News stories announcing they are to take place will be followed by speculation, leaks and further details, all before the events actually happen.

Stage 2: News event or activity
This is the pivotal point in the lifecycle, when the main news event or activity itself takes place. In the case of breaking 'original' news, such as a crime, death, resignation or other such incident, the lifecycle would start here.

Stage 3: Reaction and further development
Many journalists will spend a large part of each day working with what is already known in order to find a development. The aim is to take an existing story a stage further; to reveal additional information, action or

quotes that will be of relevance to the readership. The development may be new but much of the rest of the story will be background, or a rehash of what's been written before. Sometimes stories 'develop' based on people's reactions to the event – quotes provided by relevant people linked to the story in some way, be it as a direct participant or an industry expert. There can also be further development on the facts of the story itself. This process of development and reaction can carry on for some time, getting reaction to the reaction to the development, and so on.

Stage 4: Anniversary
Just when you thought it was all over, our desire to measure the passing of our lives demands that a story is revisited one year, ten years, 50 years or 100 years after the original news event.

Features

"It is hard news that catches readers. Features hold them."
Lord Northcliffe (1865-1922), British publisher

A feature is an opportunity to explore an issue in more detail. Constructed around case studies, data and interviews, features have a strong narrative thread and are presented in a way that allows the individual voice of the journalist to emerge.

The most common kind of feature is the news backgrounder, which provides a more detailed look at some aspect of a recent news story. For instance, the announcement that researchers have found a new drug treatment for cancer, funded in part by money raised by cancer charities, could provide the basis for the following features, depending on the publication in question:

- Positive piece looking at the potential impact of the new drug and the lives it could save, featuring case studies of people whose lives have been prolonged as a result of previous drug developments.
- Positive piece linking fundraising activities by the general public to the development of the new drug and lives being saved.
- Negative piece covering the cost of the new drug and how it's too expensive for the NHS to use, featuring criticism and complaint from relevant experts about failures of government to properly fund health care in the UK.

- Negative piece investigating cancer drug development; why, despite so much investment, more drugs like this new one aren't being developed (quicker); what's working/what's not; whether big pharma and cancer charities are focusing their efforts in the right way; areas where more funding is needed.

Features do not have to be news driven. Indeed, features provide a good opportunity to cover issues that perhaps do not make strong 'hard news' items. For instance, a charity has been working with families affected by domestic violence. The results of its services have been positive, but the number of people they have supported is too small to warrant a big headline. A feature looking at the challenges facing families is a suitable way to cover this story instead – with the caveat that it will need very strong 'triumph over tragedy' (or indeed just 'tragedy') case stories for it to work.

Longer-form features within print publications can often be called 'The essay'. These tend to be found in more serious magazines and offer the writer an opportunity to research and reflect in detail on a subject, be that poverty, immigration or other topical issues.

The qualities of a good feature are the same as with news: they need to be interesting and relevant for the reader, and contain a mixture of strong case studies, data and quotes that allow the story to be presented in a way that adds colour and depth for the reader/viewer. They will delve into the who, what, why, when and how without losing sight of the narrative.

Opinion columns

"What you see is news, what you know is background, what you feel is opinion."

Lester Markel (1894-1977), American journalist

Opinion pieces help create the tone and atmosphere of the publication or website, which in turn contributes to reader loyalty. From the likes of Katie Hopkins and Rod Liddle, both well known for their outspoken commentary of current affairs, to political journalists giving their views on the latest developments from Westminster, to industry leaders giving their perspective on a particular business challenge, the media is littered with opinion.

The volume of opinion pieces has increased further since the advent of the internet and the demand for new content 24 hours a day, seven days a week. Editors are usually crying out for good opinion pieces and so there is a wealth of opportunity for charities to pitch suggestions out. But what makes them good?

A good op-ed, as they are known in media circles, will have the following qualities:

1. Be very opinionated
Although being mild-mannered, tactful and diplomatic are superb qualities in some circumstances, they are not qualities journalists are looking for in an opinion piece. As with 'what is news' the clue is in the title. It's an opinion piece. So be opinionated.

2. Be timely or early
This links back to the life-cycle of news (above). If you can link your comment piece to something that just has happened or is about to happen then it is more likely to be published than a piece commenting on something that happened three weeks ago.

3. Demonstrate your expertise
Your experience within a particular field is what gives you the authority to have an opinion on it. So use it to your advantage.

4. Tell readers something they didn't already know
As with news and indeed any kind of content, it's vitally important that it adds something new and fresh. Otherwise it's just boring and won't be run. This means keeping your audience in mind at all times.

5. Be focused
Unlike news which needs to feature the what, where, when, why and how, an op-ed tends just to focus on one of these questions – perhaps the why? Or the how? By doing so, the writer can use the op-ed to make a single point, providing unique insight, analysis and colour to an on-going debate.

Interviews (or profiles)

The aim of an interview piece is to provide an insight into someone's life. This person will be of interest to the readership. Celebrity gossip magazines therefore will focus on celebrity interviews, while industry trade magazines will be looking for leaders within their sector.

There are many different ways in which an interview can be presented.

They can be written in first or third person; quotes can be woven into features that are supplemented with additional information; they can be presented as a Q&A (question and answer format), a case study or as a day or week in the life of the subject.

The use of celebrities within media activities

A well-thought through, appropriate celebrity partnership can of course offer many benefits. Personal appearances at events and in videos, interviews with top journalists, and supportive quotes for press releases, blogs and shareable social media posts are just a few of the ways in which these relationships can support a PR strategy.

However, for every benefit they bring, celebrities can also bring challenges and risk, and in extreme circumstances, can create press coverage for your organisation for all the wrong reasons.

So how can you assess whether this is a path down which you want to travel?

First, you need to decide which celebrity is appropriate for your organisation. Ideally they will have some connection to your cause and therefore be able to speak genuinely and from an informed perspective. They should also be relevant to your target audience. Pop stars and TV presenters might be attractive to younger audiences whereas politicians and famous business leaders might be more appropriate for wealthy or professional audiences.

Can you deliver for them? Celebrities frequently use involvement in charitable causes as a means by which to generate positive PR for themselves. If you won't be able to secure the type and breadth of coverage they demand then your chances of developing a partnership with them will be limited.

Do you have the capacity to manage the relationship? The bigger the name, the more demanding the relationship will be. Conversely, how much time you will receive from them will be dependent upon their commitments, and it may be that they are unavailable just at the very moment you need them.

Will you be able to handle it if it all goes wrong? Celebrities fall in and out of favour all the time, and regularly disgrace themselves by acting inappropriately. Associating with someone whose sex life and drug taking habits have become frontpage news could have an adverse impact upon your brand.

Finally, using a celebrity does not guarantee press coverage. You will still need all the usual components of a compelling story.

Research and reports

Journalists are hungry for data. Whether it's the fact that Brits spend more money on cheese each year than they do on good causes, the latest data on cancer survival rates or the amount of money spent on salaries, journalists love a good statistic.

Data has value as it helps make sense of the world. There is so much information available and so much 'reporting', be it by journalists, citizen journalists, eye-witnesses, commentators etc, it can be difficult to understand what should be retained and what should be disregarded. Data is used to create deeper insights into what is happening and how it might affect us. It can turn the abstract into something everyone can understand – such as how the new fundraising preference service will impact upon levels of charity donations.

Research can also help you substantiate your claims. It is all very well you saying that mothers are discriminated against in the workplace but if you can't back that view up then it won't have any credibility and is unlikely to gain traction.

Research could be in the form of academic scholarly research, online surveys, field surveys, focus groups or telephone surveys. It could be conducted by your organisation or in partnership with a market research or polling company such as Censuswide, YouGov or Ipsos Mori.

By reviewing the data you hold and finding the hidden stories within it, you can help create new and exciting stories about your work and the causes you support.

Once you have your research, there are a number of factors that are important to ensure pick up by journalists.

- Sample size: if the report is based on a survey it needs to have at least 1,000 respondents, if not more. Sometimes smaller sample sizes of a few hundred will be accepted; but the larger the better, particularly if you are gunning for national coverage.
- Key messages: make sure your headline stats are very clear and apparent within the executive summary. Journalists are busy. They don't have the time or the inclination to spend ages reading reports looking for the most important information. Make it easy for them. If it takes them until page 8 to figure out what the story is then you've lost the battle.
- Send the full report over to the journalist, highlighting the key facts in the body of the email. Don't just send the top line of a story

and ask them to call you for more details. They won't.

- Think about when you want the report to run, and how much time it will take the journalist to create a story based on your finding and then use appropriate embargoes. For example, morning bulletins and breakfast programmes are always keen to set the news agenda by covering the most fresh and up-to-date stories. By setting a midnight embargo, it can allow them to do this by giving them the space to set the story up in advance.

Oxfam's use of research

Oxfam offers a great example of how to use research and reports to secure media coverage. Senior press officer, **Melanie Kramers**, explains how.

Oxfam is a massive organisation with lots going on at all times, including the publication of research and reports. Usually they fall into one of two camps.

The first is reports based on the international development programmes we deliver, which aim to share the results and learnings from our experiences, such as empowering women in Mozambique or supporting farmers in Kenya. These can be quite technical and are often aimed at specialist and policy audiences.

The second is reports that are used to support a specific campaign. At any time we might have two or three big campaigns running, such as on climate change or tackling economic inequality. In this instance, we'd be looking to use the reports as a way of raising awareness of the issues and to provide the evidence base and potential solutions. It is this latter category that tends to be more newsworthy.

Producing and publishing the report is a collaborative process. Once we have identified that there is an evidence gap or that we need something new to say about an issue all teams have to feed into a 'Terms of Reference'. This helps us ensure that everyone understands what the purpose of the report is and what we hope to achieve with it. If getting media coverage is a key objective then the press team will be more involved so we can make it as strong as possible.

To have any chance of being picked up by a journalist, the report needs to include something new and interesting. It needs to offer a USP (unique selling point) and add value to what is already out there.

This means we have to strongly challenge the research and policy teams to explain what's new about we are saying. The most important thing is to tell a good story, and that needs a strong top line – often based on a killer statistic that will generate debate. For example, we've got a good track record for securing mainstream coverage around the annual Davos economic forum, most recently when we revealed that the world's richest one per cent of people will own more than everyone else put together by 2016.

One way to test the story's strength is to come up with potential headlines at the start. Therefore, it's essential the media team feeds into the report from the outset. If you get a ready-made report landing on your desk that makes the key newsworthy elements: (a headline and new fact, analysis or statistic) it can be difficult or even impossible for you to do anything with it.

In addition to the story, we have to think about timing and the hook. If it's the wrong time or other things are happening it can be difficult to get journalists to take notice. We might use an event such as Davos or a meeting of the World Bank as a hook, or an anniversary, such as six months on from an earthquake.

When we pitch, we make sure we focus on that top line. We write a snappy, concise press release that includes an emotive quote and make sure we have spokespeople available for interviews. What we don't do is just send them the report and ask them to read it. Journalists are so busy that we have to make it really easy for them to identify the most exciting part of the report.

There are multiple benefits to taking this kind of approach to media relations. It is a way of showing the depth and breadth of the work we do; it enhances our reputation as a credible and experienced organisation that knows what it's talking about; and it's a way of raising the profile of key issues that are important to us.

It can also help us gain new supporters – most members of the public probably aren't going to read a long report from cover to cover but a newspaper story will indicate to them that we're making a difference to people's lives. High value donors who prefer to take an evidence-based approach to their funding may use these reports to help them make a decision about where to direct donations. Some of our reports make more headlines than others but when the story and timing come together successfully we can see the impact.'

The letters page

The letters page allows an editor to demonstrate a breadth of views and can open up debate on a particular subject area. Most national and regional newspapers and magazines have a letters page and some even reproduce it within their digital output.

Having a letter published can be a good opportunity to raise the profile of your cause and get your point of view across on a particular issue.

Editors receive hundreds of letters and emails from people every day so you will need to work hard to ensure that your letter is strong enough to be selected. It should be clear, concise and to the point, of no more than 150 words unless in exceptional circumstances (editors like letters that don't require much editing), be authoritative but measured, and shouldn't include anything that could be misunderstood – once it's published there is no turning back.

Audio visual

Words are important. But so too is photography, audio and video, and therefore these shouldn't be neglected when thinking about what you have to offer journalists. Being able to deliver an audio visual tool alongside a story will get you extra marks as they are a great way to open up different ways to tell a story and offer greater context to the audience.

Images

As the old adage goes, a picture tells a thousand words, and no journalist will run a story of more than a few hundred words without a picture. Note, though, that many media outlets commission their own photographers or use images from photo libraries such as Getty, so check first to ensure you're not wasting your time.

As with copy, the picture has to be interesting (ie not a photo of your team holding a cheque) and it has to be high quality. Some key qualities of a good image are as follows:

Image quality: The photo should be of print quality, meaning it will need to offer high resolution and a sharpness of image for the size it is to be used at. Colour should be strong with no fuzziness, reflection or fringing. The image has to be the right orientation for the layout – be that portrait or landscape, with uncluttered space available for headlines and intros to be placed.

Story: The photo should tell the story in its own way, whether by providing a historical or of-the-moment dimension, by the subjects being arranged in an interesting way, or by adding a special something to the piece. Facial expression can play an important role here.

Video

It isn't just broadcasters for whom video is important. As websites have become more sophisticated and it has become easier to embed video, video has become an increasingly important part of an online journalist's toolbox. As with other forms of content, journalists are willing to take video content from other people as long as it is relevant and usable.

Structure: The first five seconds are the most important when it comes to video. If you haven't grabbed the viewers' attention in this time they are unlikely to watch it all the way through.

The end is just as important as the beginning. Ideally the video should tell a short story (about two minutes long) with a conclusion or reveal at the end. And don't forget to include a link so that viewers can find out more if they want to.

Quality: The larger the file size, the longer the video will take to load – which again can be off-putting, so use small files that load fast. A steady camera is important so as not to make viewers feel sick, which also means keeping use of the zoom to a minimum.

Audio

With no visuals to act as a guide, audio (or podcast, as it is commonly known) has to work much harder to tell a story but can be more effective as the audience has to rely on their imagination. It can also be listened to while on the go, unlike reading or watching video.

A podcast is a digital audio file, made from a recording. Like any audio file – a song for instance, or an audiobook – it can be downloaded from the internet, and listened to on a computer, digital music player, or phone. In practice though, it's more than just an audio file. Podcasts are usually created as part of a series, and/or used as a means of ongoing regular communication, such as a radio show. A podcast can take the form of a debate, an informal conversation, an interview, an episode of a story, or even a monologue answering questions and queries to provide a bank of helpful information for listeners. They tend to be longer than a video – the optimum time being between 15 and 20 minutes long. The word 'podcast' gives a clue to this: it's a combination of the word 'iPod' – a portable media player – with 'broadcast'.

My colleague Viv Oyolu of AudioByte believes podcasts to be a powerful communication tool because many people find it easier to assimilate information aurally – hence why students still go to lectures, and talk radio shows remain popular.

Some media outlets offer podcasts as part of their package of content. They may be on the hunt for expert commentators to interview so this should be factored into your strategic planning.

Chapter 4 in a nutshell

- Journalists are not only interested in negative or sensationalist stories. They are only interested good stories which interest, surprise or shock people, and tell them something they didn't already know.
- People like to read/hear about other people. They like stories they can relate to or about issues they can talk about. Human interest stories, with strong real-life case studies at their heart, should be an important part of your PR strategy.
- News is important but it's not the only option available to you. Consider if and how you can contribute to features and opinion pieces, and don't forget to include other media such as audio, video and photography.
- A good rule of thumb to apply against any story or case study is the 'So what?' test. Will anyone but you actually care about the story you're pitching? How does it add value to their lives? Why do they need to know this information? Does it tell them something they don't already know?

5
HOW TO PITCH SUCCESSFULLY

There are a number of ways in which you can increase the chances of your stories being picked up. First and foremost, it's about providing good ideas for content.

Sources of ideas

Providing a regular flow of relevant and usable ideas is one way to make yourself indispensable to a journalist. But where do these ideas come from?

1) The diary: The diary is the source of many an idea for a story. Indeed, many editorial offices start their day or their week with a look at what is coming up. The diary will contain details of all regular meetings and events, press conferences, visits by politicians or celebrities, anniversaries of events and industry announcements. By maintaining your own diary you can ensure you are on top of all important dates that might require a response from your organisation and you can plan ahead – making sure that you are one step ahead of the journalists and can meet their tight deadlines.

2) Your own work: You know what the most recent development is, or which issues are making the work of your organisation harder or easier to achieve. Think about what you could pitch as a news story or feature idea, but remember it needs to offer something new and surprising (see Chapter 4 for more on the different types of content).

3) Current issues: Current issues of publications and recent broadcasts should be reviewed for relevant stories on which you might be able to give a comment or provide a journalist with more information that can be used as a 'development'. The letters pages and comment boxes are also a good place to look; an individual may have raised an issue that you can respond to. This is known as 'hijacking'. Story hijacking has been part of the PR toolbox for many years and allows organisations to piggyback on high profile anniversaries, new legislation, industry developments etc. However, for it to be a success, charities still need to have something relevant, valuable and interesting to say.

4) Comparable magazines/shows: Trade magazines are often used by newspapers looking for news and developments that they can translate into stories relevant for their readership. Science and technology provide a good example of this, with papers in medical journal *The Lancet* for instance being frequently picked up by national broadcasters. Equally, the local press is scanned by the regionals, and newspapers are scanned by magazine journalists. Savvy media teams will be working in the same way, looking for ideas they can pitch to other journalists.

5) Back-issues: Back issues of relevant publications can be mined for stories that have a forthcoming anniversary, or would make a good past-present comparison. These back issues can be found within the publication's online archive, or at the British Library, which holds copies of every single publication ever issued.

6) Anniversaries and awareness weeks: Remembering significant events, such as natural disasters, the launch of a government initiative or the death of a celebrity, can make a good peg on which to hang story ideas; as too can awareness days/weeks and months (see case study below).

7) Social media: Twitter and Facebook can be valuable sources of news and ideas from specialist accounts, be this of the publication itself or key commentators within particular sectors.

Awareness weeks

Dyslexia Awareness Week sees many of the dyslexia organisations in the UK, and also some internationally, working together in the same time period to raise awareness of what dyslexia is and how it affects people. **Nicola Amoroso**, marketing and communications manager at Dyslexia Action, explains how it works.

Awareness events can be important instigators of conversations about topics that some people would otherwise find difficult to – or may not think to – discuss.

Dyslexia Awareness Week has been a very positive experience for Dyslexia Action in recent years. By putting real stories of real people in the public eye, it helps to create greater understanding of the difficulties associated with dyslexia, and to increase empathy towards those who have it.

Awareness days or weeks provide relevant media with an opportunity to cover a particular cause they might not usually give attention to. To take advantage of this, it is important to have briefed spokespeople about the key messages you want to communicate and prepared case studies ahead of time so you can act fast when the time comes.

It's possible to create much more noise around an awareness day or week if you join forces with other like-minded charities that share the same passions and beliefs. Each organisation can work to its particular strengths, which when combined will create much more impact than if you were to work alone. This can be particularly beneficial if another charity has a relationship with a section of the media that you do not.

An important factor in the success of an awareness campaign is participation. Dyslexia Action works with employers, educational establishments, parents and individuals affected by dyslexia, and we encourage all these groups to get involved during Dyslexia Awareness Week. This means we need to focus our media activity on those media outlets that are relevant to this audience. It is also important to make it as easy as possible for people to participate, so we offer suggestions as to what they might like to do. For example, last year we provided schools with information on how to teach a dyslexia-friendly lesson.

Awareness Week dos/don'ts

Do:

- Inviting a local journalist to shadow a volunteer for the day so they can write about the experiences.
- Plan ahead and co-ordinate stories – if the awareness event is spanning several days, plan content with a different focus for each day.
- Give the awareness day/week a theme to keep ideas fresh. For example, the theme for Dyslexia Awareness Week 2015 was "Making Sense of Dyslexia" while for 2014 it was "Dyslexia Matters...".

Don't:

- Confuse your audience – decide your key messages and stick to them.
- Overstretch resources – less good content and coverage is better than lots of poor quality content.
- Send a representative in to a situation that they are not confident in – live TV/radio can be daunting for some!
- Waste resources – consider what you are likely to achieve and the benefits it will bring and plan accordingly.

How to pitch

The challenge a media team will face is convincing an editor or journalist to take their ideas. So how can you make sure they love what you offer them?

1. Come up with suitable ideas that are targeted carefully at their niche. Is your story what their reader/viewer wants to read/watch? Does it extend their knowledge? Is it surprising or shocking in any way?
2. Approach the right person. Do some research into which journalists have previously covered similar types of stories; find out who makes decisions about running the type of content you are pitching.
3. Consider giving a journalist an exclusive. This is when you offer a story to one journalist either alone or first, so that they are the ones who break the story.

Factors to consider when deciding whether or not to offer an exclusive are:

- Is my story important/strong enough to attract the interest of the journalist?
- Who should get the exclusive (does it help you reach your target audience?)?
- What benefits will offering the exclusive bring (stronger relationship with the journalist, wider reach etc)?
- What are the potential disadvantages (the story may get dropped in favour of something else; other publications may choose not to run any follow-up stories, thus limiting coverage and reach)?

If you do decide to offer an exclusive, make sure you talk 'off the record' until the reporter agrees to the exclusive. Don't spill the beans too early. Then once the journalist has agreed, be as specific as possible about what information is exclusive and for how long, whether you will give interviews to other publications after the story has broken, etc.

4. Send a written outline via email first, and then follow it up by phone afterwards. Not the other way round. Busy people are reluctant to take calls and even if they do pick up the phone they might be too busy to pay attention to an unsolicited pitch. It's also much easier to consider an idea when it's written down first.
5. Make sure what you send is error free and well written. What you present will indicate to them whether you can write and present an argument constructively – a key determining factor as to whether your pitch will be successful or not.
6. Think about when you are sending your email or making the call. If the journalist is on deadline with an article or in the throes of getting an issue to press (also known as putting it to bed) then they are unlikely to have time to pay your pitch much attention.
7. Consider the use of embargoes. An embargo is a request by the news source that the information or news provided by that source not be published until a certain date or certain conditions have been met. It is often used so that journalists have time to prepare (but not publish) their stories ahead of an announcement being made. The understanding is that if the embargo is broken then the source will subsequently restrict access to further information, thus putting that journalist or media outlet at a disadvantage. It is considered a serious breach of trust to break an embargo and therefore it is rare. However, it is not unheard of, and some journalists will willingly break embargoes if they feel the story is worth it and if they believe that you need them more than they need you.
8. Follow up a response. Editors and journalists receive hundreds of emails every day. They may have missed yours. Chase, but try not to sound too desperate in the process, and certainly do not pester. This will only serve to irritate the journalist.
9. If pitching feature or blog ideas then feel free to pitch to multiple journalists from different outlets at the same time. However, if you secure a piece then out of courtesy you should let the others know While you might not mind multiple publications running your article, the editors will and you'll end up with a black mark against your name.
10. If your pitch is accepted, stick to the brief. Deadlines are sacrosanct. If you miss the deadline then you may miss the print or broadcast date and time, leaving the editor with a gaping hole. They will not be happy. The only occasion where extensions might be available is

if an external event has taken place that means you are unable to access the key information required – such as a government announcement being delayed. But don't leave this to the last minute. If you need to negotiate an extension do so in plenty of time.

11. Sending in copy – the basic rules are to supply it in Microsoft Word or in the body of an email. Definitely not as a PDF. Images must be high resolution Jpegs or Tifs. Do not insert an image into a Word document as it will be unusable for print. Again, check first whether it is necessary to provide images.

Press packs

A press pack or media kit can be a helpful addition to any PR's armoury. This is a pre-packaged set of promotional materials about your organisation that is distributed to members of the media either in its entirety or in sections, depending on what's required. It should also be made available to download from your website, thus making it easy for journalists to access when researching stories.

The usual components of a press kit include some or all of the following:

Organisation overview: This is the place to sum up your charity and its work so that someone who hasn't heard of you before will understand what it is you do and the difference you make. It should be no longer than two-sides of A4, and should be neatly spaced so that it is easy to read and digest.

Key biographies: This should include your chief executive and any other team members who act as spokespeople for your organisation. It should highlight their key areas of expertise and specialist subject areas within no more than three paragraphs of text.

Press releases: If you're sending a press pack to a journalist for a specific reason then you should include the press release that relates to the issue in hand. If the press pack is available online then it should include all your latest press releases. This will help save you and interested journalists much time and effort.

FAQs: A question and answer factsheet can be a useful way to illustrate particular aspects of your work, highlight your impact and differentiate your organisation from other similar charities. Ask your supporter services team, if you have one, for typical questions that frequently arise.

Images, video and audio: This could include logos, photos and videos of your work in action, and key spokespeople. Many charities choose to put these behind a password protected wall on their website so that they can see who is downloading them and retain some control over how they are used. Don't forget to include details of any photo credits and captions. Everything should be in high-resolution to ensure it is of print and broadcast quality.

Contact details: It might sound obvious but charities frequently forget to include a section telling journalists whom they should contact for more information. You should include phone numbers and email addresses for your spokespeople, public relations person or a designated staff member who handles media requests.

The role of press releases

"News is what somebody somewhere wants to suppress;
all the rest is advertising."
Lord Northcliffe (1865-1922), British publisher

There is a school of thought within some camps of journalists – as indicated by Lord Northcliffe's quote above – that press releases are nothing but PR puff and as such they promptly delete them. At the other end of the spectrum are those who take a more lackadaisical approach and will use a press release in its entirety rather than rewriting it. Somewhere in the middle are those journalists who might use a press release as the foundation of a news story, with additional information added from their own research, or who use them as inspiration for features and blogs.

Press releases can be great when you are announcing your own news but less effective when responding to other people's, such as a government announcement or industry development – in the main this is down to the length of time they take to write and get signed off. Charity PRs have to be reactive, fast and flexible: if you want a journalist to include your thoughts on the Budget then you have to get your comments over to them as soon as the relevant section of the Budget has been announced. In instances such as these a two-paragraph quote can be much quicker and easier to write and get signed off.

Don't be disappointed if the story you've put forward doesn't see the light of day. Ultimately it's a journalist's job to keep their editors – rather than you or your charity – happy, so don't be offended if your press release isn't used. Even if the journalist expresses interest and writes the story, it might not always run. Big news changes all agendas and things will get bumped or spiked.

That said, it is important to balance the amount of effort required with the possibility of success. To do this, it is essential to check whether your story passes the 'So what?' test and is actually something people will want to read about (see page 38).

How to write a press release

- Headline – a great headline (also used as the subject line of the email) to grab the attention of the journalist is key.
- Date and time – including details of any embargo.
- First paragraph – after the headline it is the first paragraph that journalists will read to see if they are interested in the story. The rule here is to include the 5Ws: who, what, where, why and when.
- Subsequent paragraphs – this is where you include the supporting information for the story. It should be kept clear and concise. Every word matters so make sure that each sentence could be used to communicate the story.
- Quotes – include one or two quotes that provide further insight into the story.
- Editor's notes – this is where contact information and any further information that might be relevant to the story is included, such as links to your website, report, case studies etc.
- Keep it brief – one page is ideal, two pages is the absolute maximum.
- Make it easy to read – use 1.5 or double spacing throughout.
- Include the press release within the body of the email. Don't attach it purely as a PDF; no one will open it.

Here is a bad and a good example of a press contact from Amber Valley Angels, promoting a recent event the charity held.

Bad example

Hello Carol,
We held an event last week. Would you like to cover it?
Bob Gelding, our chief executive, talked about our services, while the head of social services at the council talked about the difference we made to older people in the local area. If you want I can send you the details. We would love to get some coverage about our work.
Best wishes,
Denise from the PR team

Good example

Amber Valley Angels offers a "lifeline" to vulnerable local people
10 March 2016, for immediate release

Amber Valley Angels offers a "lifeline" to vulnerable local people, delegates to an Amber Valley council event heard today.

Bob Gelding, chief executive of Amber Valley Angels, said: "Amber Valley Angels' network of 150 volunteers delivers vital services day and night to 3,000 disabled, infirm and older people throughout our region. They are a lifeline to these people who otherwise would not see or speak to anyone else for weeks at a time."

Tina Jarvis, chief executive of Amber Valley Council, said: "We applaud Amber Valley Angels and its volunteers for the great work they do. Their dedication and support not only brighten up many people's lives and show them that people care, but they also prevent many from being admitted into hospital, saving our council around £100,000 each year."

Theresa Gordon, 96 years old and a local resident, said: "I don't know what I'd do without my Angel. She brings me my shopping every Wednesday and we have a lovely chat over a cup of tea and a biscuit. She's the only person I see all week."

The event was held at 10am today to mark the 10th anniversary of the charity, and was attended by 100 guests from local businesses and community groups.

Editor's notes:
Amber Valley Angels delivers practical and emotional support to disabled, infirm and older people in the Amber Valley region. For more information, visit www.ambervalleyangels.org.uk

For interviews and further information, contact Judith Bridges on 01773 55555

High-res photos are available to download from this link here: www.ambervalleyangels.org.uk/press

Distributing press releases

Relying on personal contacts and relationships as a means by which to distribute press releases can be the most successful way to secure press coverage, but it can be onerous.

Paid-for distribution services, such as Gorkana and PR Newswire enable you to send press releases out in bulk to carefully targeted lists of journalists. This can be a very cost-effective way of reaching a large number of journalists in one fell swoop. They also offer media monitoring and analysis tools, which can help you measure the effectiveness of your activities. However, they can be expensive for charities that do not produce much news and so it might be more affordable to enlist the support of a PR agency that has access to the service and can send out releases on your behalf instead.

Another distribution option is the 'wires', such as Press Association (PA) or Associated Press (AP), which are sent out live to news desks around the world via satellite and accessed by many news journalists. A recent survey of British journalists found that 67% use the wires, with 37% using them daily. According to this group, 54% found PR Newswire the most valuable, with PA coming in at 38%.

There are two ways in which to get your story featured on the wires. The first is by contacting the PA newsdesk with your story directly. If they decide to take your story, which is by no means a given, they may alter the focus of your press release to highlight what the news team considers to be the main story. The story is then circulated on the news wires and the content is attributed to PA. Journalists will often pick up on this content because it has already been 'approved' by the PA news team.

The second is to pay for your press release to be fed into the PA news wire. For example, PR Newswire, which co-owns PA, can feed your release, intact, onto the PA wire. It may not garner as much initial interest as a PA-written story, but if the content is strong then it is likely to get picked up.

In both cases, there are no guarantees that your story will be picked up. It has still got to offer great news content and is still vulnerable to the whims of journalists and how busy or slow the news environment is at that time.

Free tools

Journalisted.com is a website that contains free access to journalists' details while *Press Gazette* and Journalism.com offer freelance directories containing details of journalists and their subject areas, all of which can be helpful when building media lists.

Another helpful free service is AskCharity, which is operated by CharityComms and designed to help journalists and charities work together. Journalists can use it to find case studies, spokespeople and information from a wide range of charities. Charities can use it to build their media contacts and coverage. For example, a national journalist wants a case study on a young person who has been in jail and suffers from depression. They submit their request online, which is distributed to all those charities registered with AskCharity which work with young people, and in the fields of criminal justice and mental health. They are then able to contact the journalist should they have a suitable case study available.

Using the wires

Anaphylaxis Campaign has been able to expand its reach by using PR Newswire. **Sarah Birkett-Wendes**, PR and communications manager, explains how.

The Anaphylaxis Campaign is a charity that supports those affected by severe allergy. It was set up 21 years ago by a group of parents who were directly affected by the condition. The group lead was journalist David Reading OBE who tragically lost his daughter, Sarah, in 1994 to anaphylaxis.

The charity, like most patient groups, was born from an unmet need of support. It grew rapidly in a blaze of media interest driven by David Reading who used his media skills to gain publicity and awareness for better diagnosis and catering care. David's daughter Sarah knew about her allergy to peanuts – however she was unaware the dish she ordered while eating out contained peanut.

I joined the charity in 2012 at which point it had very limited media contacts. An Excel spreadsheet of around 200 contacts formed the basis of most of our campaigns, supported by internet searches, meaning we then had to individually email our press releases to each journalist – a long and laborious task.

I knew from previous experience that if we could gain access to a media database this process would be automated and would also enable us to reach many more media contacts. We would also be able to segment and target different media depending on the story. This would then expand our reach considerably.

Research showed that PR Newswire was our best option – the system is straightforward to use and its lists are updated regularly. I put together a report to take to the board to get the annual cost signed off.

Our success in gaining coverage since having access to PR Newswire's database has been extensive. We have been successful in securing national coverage, including across broadsheets such as the *Daily Telegraph*, and regional coverage. The Campaign runs support groups up and down the country and so PR Newswire is very helpful in enabling us to reach local press in these areas. In addition, journalists now know about the Anaphylaxis Campaign from having seen our press releases and we get a lot more direct calls to our press office.

At the same time we have increased activity on our social media channels. This, combined with our more targeted and extended press activity has combined to increase the number of hits to our website from 7,000 a month in Jan 2012 to 60,000 a month in January 2015.

> I would recommend that all small and medium charities should consider subscribing to a media database and use it regularly – the awareness gained is priceless.

Media partnerships (paid-for and earned)

PR agencies and media planners typically organise channels into four groups that each offer distinct characteristics: paid-for, earned, shared and owned (PESO).

Paid-for media includes advertising and marketing channels that you pay for, including TV, radio, cinema, outdoor, press advertising, direct mail and online.

Earned media is that secured as a result of the relationship you have with journalists, bloggers and other key influencers (the focus of this guide).

Owned includes your organisational website, plus any other media space over which you have full ownership and control, such as shop fronts, or leaflets in service centres.

Shared means social channels such as Facebook, Twitter, YouTube etc, as well as referrals and word of mouth.

The lines between these can sometimes be blurred, such as when media partnerships are put in place. These can incorporate some or all of the four groups. For instance:

- A newspaper charity appeal, such as *The Times* Christmas Appeal (earned)
- A special television programme or series, such as the ITV show *Paul O'Grady: For the Love of Dogs*, which is produced in partnership with Battersea Dogs and Cats Home (earned and owned)
- A special supplement and event, such as the former partnership between Medical Aid for Palestinians and the *New Statesman*, which involved party conference fringe events and an eight-page report (paid-for)
- A popular blogger or vlogger agreeing to mention a charity in someway, or participating in a charity fundraising or volunteering opportunity which they then write about/feature within a vlog (earned or possibly paid-for, depending on the blogger/vlogger)

- A multi-platform sponsorship deal involving multiple partners that stretches across a media outlet, the charity's own digital channels and that of a corporate partner (paid-for, owned, shared).

Whether paid-for or not, the key to successful media partnerships is to ensure that they are mutually beneficial. This means ensuring they are the right fit: will they help you reach the right people at the right time with the right message, and does the publication or broadcaster share in your values (women's rights charities for example might find it inappropriate to partner with *The Sun* because of its Page 3)?

If a media outlet can identify multiple benefits, such as increased sales, lots of engaging content and their CSR box ticked, then charity media partnerships can often be arranged for free or via an application process. Increasingly though, as publications look to secure revenue streams, there will be a fee involved. These can still create considerable value for the charity partner, not least because paid-for media partnerships usually offer the client (the charity) much more control over the published content and its messaging than those partnerships that are free.

If you do take on a paid-for media partnership, make sure you're not just working with the sales team. These can place too much emphasis on 'salesy' content, which can be off-putting to readers. Editorial teams can help charities create content that is not overtly branded but that still communicates all the key messages while at the same time strengthening your reputation and authority. But don't forget to abide by any rules and regulations, such as those that stipulate sponsored content must be labeled at such.

Partnerships don't have to just involve a charity and a media outlet. Other brands can also get involved, such as celebrity or consumer brands that have a synergy with the cause and the media audience. For example, a healthy food brand and diabetes charity may work jointly on a paid-for media partnership with a popular women's lifestyle magazine. The collaboration could include healthy recipes, case studies about women with diabetes, exclusive interviews with celebrities affected by diabetes, discount vouchers towards healthy food items, downloadable diet and exercise plans from the charity's website and special exclusive events only available to magazine subscribers. The media outlet receives an income and content, the food brand encourages target audiences to try its product, and the charity reaches target audiences with messages about the role of healthy eating in preventing diabetes: an all-round win.

Media partnerships

Contact the Elderly was selected as one of four charities featured in *The Times* Christmas Appeal 2015. **Sarah Miles** is from Stand Agency, which worked with the charity on the application and subsequent appeal.

As the only national charity solely dedicated to tackling loneliness and social isolation among older people, Contact the Elderly is often seen as a lifeline. Supported by a network of volunteers, the charity offers a regular and vital friendship link via its monthly Sunday afternoon tea parties for older people aged 75 and over, who live alone.

2015 was a special year for Contact the Elderly, as the charity was celebrating its Golden Jubilee. It wanted to end the year in style and so we applied for *The Times* Christmas appeal.

The Times wanted a written application, and set out the instructions clearly. The submission gave background details on the charity – how it was formed, its progress over the years and detailed information about specific projects, case studies and story ideas.

More than 200 charities also applied, but only four were selected by the newspaper. Contact the Elderly was one of them – chosen because of its long-standing commitment to eradicating loneliness and social isolation, as well as the evidence that its monthly tea parties make a significant difference to people's lives.

Over the Christmas and New Year period, the newspaper and online editions featured stories that highlighted the charity's work and explained the impact its service has. The stories and case studies from the tea party groups up and down the country demonstrated how volunteers change lives by giving up just a few hours of their time each month, as well as the power of regular face-to-face contact.

Looking back, the appeal was a great success. Contact the Elderly was featured in eight national news stories in just one month. As a result, donations have increased; the number of older people reaching out for help has increased, as has the number of volunteers. We also know that when approaching journalists at *The Times* in the future, they will be familiar with the charity and its brilliant work and therefore will be our first stop for Contact the Elderly's next big announcement.

So, what made our application stand out from others?

We believe our application was successful because we demonstrated how Contact the Elderly's solution worked in reality and explained how it was tackling one of the biggest social challenges facing the UK. We made use of statistics, case studies and impact analysis to demonstrate this and clearly showed how we met all the criteria.

The human-interest angle was key to winning a place on the appeal. It was clear from our application that the eight emotive story ideas we provided would translate into readable and inspiring stories.

Top tips for other charities? Be very specific in your application, make sure you meet all the criteria requests and back up your claims with hard evidence – both impactful case studies and powerful statistics.

Chapter 5 in a nutshell

- Identify the right journalist and pitch to them at the right time and in the right way. Tailor your ideas to their needs, email over all the key details together, and follow up with them in a way that won't make them feel hassled.
- Relying on personal contacts and relationships as a means by which to distribute press releases can be the most successful way to secure press coverage, but it can be onerous. Paid-for distribution services, such as Gorkana and PR Newswire, and free services such as AskCharity and Journalisted.com, can all be helpful when building media lists and distributing to many journalists at one time.
- Don't be disappointed if the story you've put forward doesn't see the light of day. Even if the journalist expresses interest and writes the story, it might not always run. Big news changes all agendas and things will get bumped or spiked.
- Paid-for media partnerships shouldn't be disregarded as they can offer much more control over the published content and its messaging than those partnerships that are free.

6
OTHER IMPORTANT RULES TO TRY NOT TO BREAK

It isn't just good content that will help you build strong relationships with journalists. There are a number of other factors at play that are important to take into consideration.

House style

This is a set of rules about the presentation style of editorial or broadcast material, including the finer points of copy editing, such as whether numbers over 10 should be words or figures, whether news-stand should be hyphenated, whether job titles in captions and credits, such as Managing Director, should be capitalised or not. Its purpose is to ensure conformity, which is important for the credibility of the brand and to gain the trust of the readers/viewers. It is not necessary for PRs to get a publication's house style correct to the letter, but a broad awareness of its tone and stance is extremely helpful.

The Economist's style guide is perhaps the most famous of all. This can be purchased from book shops or downloaded online, and offers a good rule of thumb for charity PRs to apply to their own copy. The *Guardian* and *Observer's* house style is also available online, as is the *Telegraph's* style book. It can be interesting to compare and contrast how different publications do things and how their different political stances have a bearing on house style.

House style can also help set the tone of the publication or broadcaster. Sometimes this tone can be deliberate to give readers/viewers a sense of belonging – such as magazines or shows for young people that use alliteration, abandon the use of second syllables (fave instead of favourite), or use slang (LOL to represent laugh-out-loud).

Other examples include *The New Yorker*, *The Spectator* or *New Statesman*, which are different from a newspaper or lifestyle magazine – the tone often being authoritative or irreverent. Likewise other magazines use tone and style to show commitment to readers: *Slimming World* magazine, for example, would never use the word "fat" but "overweight", nor "diet" but "healthy eating plan". These rules extend not just through its editorial but into the commercial content as well, with advertisers having to follow the same style and tone. The same principles apply across all channels, be it print, broadcast or online.

Therefore, what any good media team must do is understand the market they are writing for and adjust the style of language they use – both in written and verbal form – according to each particular audience.

The use of jargon

Another common complaint from journalists is that charities use a lot of technical language that can make copy and interviews difficult to understand, and – to be frank – quite dull.

While the refugees in Europe may be lacking an appropriate 'resettlement strategy', this phrase won't automatically be understandable by everyone, and therefore 'finding refugees new homes' may help paint a better picture in the minds of your target audience. Likewise, complex medical terms should be simplified – or better still, avoided – as much as possible. As too should phrases such as beneficiary, stakeholder and customer.

This applies no matter what form of content you are providing: never use a foreign phrase, scientific word or jargon if there is an everyday plain English equivalent.

Frequency

The frequency of publication or broadcast has a significant impact on the amount of content needed and the speed at which journalists have to work. This in turn will impact upon the opportunities available to charity PRs.

Up to the minute: News channels and news websites that publish up-to-the-minute, as-it-happens, news have a constantly rolling output of content. Often they will focus on several 'headline' stories with other relevant news being published alongside this. The majority of this will be hard news, reporting on new events, supplemented with some pre-planned preview stories and reaction/new developments (see the lifecycle of news, page 41). Therefore any news being pitched to this type of outlet needs to be fresh. Even a day old and you have missed the boat.

Hourly/Daily: As above, this content tends to be driven by hard news with some analysis that adds depth and context.

Weekly/fortnightly: Magazines that publish weekly or fortnightly have a longer lead in time. While some of the content will be time sensitive, much of it will have been planned in advance. This gives PR people the opportunity to pitch in ideas throughout the production schedule. They will have a date they 'go-to-press', print overnight and be out a day or two later.

Monthly/bi-monthly: Magazines that publish monthly or even fewer times a year will have the longest lead in time of all. They will also go to print much further in advance of their publication date. This means charity PR people need to think quite a way ahead if they want to be considered by these editors. For instance, women's lifestyle magazines tend to start producing their December issues in July. So if you want a journalist to run your story on how your charity supports lonely people at Christmas you need to have pitched the idea well before summer starts.

Timings

Charity PRs often complain that journalists don't give them enough time to source everything they want – seemingly wanting everything right now (or yesterday). Case studies have to be sourced, quotes written and signed off – which cannot happen immediately when there is a chain of command to go through.

Unfortunately for you, this is something you're just going to have to deal with if you want your content to be used. Journalists have to produce their stories quickly. News reporters have to file stories at such speed because, if left too late, the news will no longer be new and it will defeat the point. Equally, journalism is expensive and so journalists will be under pressure to deliver a large amount of work in order to minimise costs. This does not give them the luxury of time and most journalists simply do not have enough hours in the day to allow interviewees and contributors lots of time to prepare.

If you want your content to be used by a journalist then you have to deliver it to the deadline they have asked for. If a journalist says they need copy by 10am on Tuesday then that is when they want it for. Not 4pm on the Wednesday. Do that and not only will you miss the boat, but you will have left a very sour taste in the mouth of the journalist who is unlikely to use you for comment or content again. If they need an interview within the next 30 minutes that is what they need. Any later will be too late.

This means charity PRs – and the spokespeople they put forward – have to be prepared. They need to be contactable after-hours, willing and able to leave meetings to take calls and participate in interviews, and to work at speed. Case studies need to be ready and waiting – not just in written form but for telephone and broadcast interviews. Anyone who is being put in front of a journalist should also have been fully briefed and provided with media training so that they are able to respond clearly and effectively to questions (see Chapter 7).

Ultimately, this also means a quick sign-off process is essential. If a piece of content or an interview has to go through three or four people before it can be signed off this is going to dramatically slow the process down. Ideally the PR will have autonomy and will be able to authorise publication themselves, rather than having to wait for the all-clear from the busy chief executive who won't be back in the office until next week.

Commissioning

When it comes to the provision of articles and comment pieces, there is nothing more frustrating for an editor than to find that the content provided has not met the brief given. If, for example, a brief says that you should provide your views on how women are being discriminated against in the workplace then that is what you should provide, not an overview of your charity and its services.

The same applies to the word count. If 600 words are commissioned, provide 600 words not 100 or 1,600.

To avoid misunderstanding, ask the person commissioning you to provide a written outline via email. It is also helpful to ask which are the essential elements of the story and which are less crucial but desirable.

If the copy does not meet the brief then it will either be sent back to you for a rewrite, or won't be used at all, which will have been a waste of your time and the editor's. The editor will also be left feeling cross that they now have to commission someone else.

Conversely, an experienced PR or writer that can be depended upon to produce copy to professional standards can quickly become an editor's best friend.

Who owns the message?

Charities work with the most vulnerable members of society so it is only right that they need to protect these people from intrusive and inappropriate media coverage. Likewise, the organisation's brand needs to be represented in a positive light to maintain and strengthen their reputation.

However, this does not mean that charities can control the way in which a journalist presents a story. I am frequently asked by charity media contacts if they can check the story before it goes out, if they can add additional content that includes their key messages, or if they can change the way I have presented the argument. The answer is – usually – no. You may find a few journalists who are willing to send a quote over for approval but it is rare and is unlikely to include the full article, nor will they be happy to make significant changes. In the main, the only way in which a charity can control the message is if they have written a piece themselves (and even then it still has to meet the brief) or have paid for a sponsored feature or advertorial.

Ultimately, the story belongs to the journalist or editor. They are making decisions all day long about stories – be this about the contents, design, layout, tone or style. The last thing they care about is whether your key message has been included or not. Also, they know their brand and their audience best. Being overly protective of the message is only going to serve to irritate them and ruin your chances of securing coverage. The best way to approach this is to work with the journalist to help them develop the best angle, and then provide them with the information they need to present that angle accurately.

To achieve all of this, the entire organisation needs to understand how the media works, not just the PR person or team. Often the stumbling blocks occur not in the media team (who will most likely be very knowledgeable about how the media works) but elsewhere within the organisation, such as in programmes teams (which often control the message and insist on the use of jargon) or within senior management. Yet those organisations where a proactive approach to the media is driven from the top end up reaping the rewards, Save the Children and Oxfam being prime examples. Centrepoint is another – a small organisation but one which punches above its weight when it comes to media coverage (see page 77).

Off the record and Chatham House rules

'Off the record' is a phrase used to highlight that a particular aspect of a conversation or statement is not meant to be part of the recorded account of a proceeding, such as an interview or court case. It is used when people need to say something that must remain unpublished and/or unattributable, for instance when relaying something that occurred in a private meeting.

The 'Chatham House rule' is usually invoked at meetings to encourage openness and the sharing of information. When a meeting or part of a meeting is held under the Chatham House rule, participants are free to use the information received, but neither the identity nor the affiliation of the speaker/s or participants may be revealed, unless specific permission is sought afterwards.

As with abiding by embargoes, it is very bad form for a journalist to violate either off the record or Chatham House rule statements and meetings. However, journalists often conflate the two, meaning off the record comments may still be used but not attributed to you. If it is absolutely essential that a particular statement not be published, it is best practice to agree terms of an interview or meeting in writing before it takes place. Or better still, don't say it in the first place.

Please note, however, there is nothing more frustrating for journalists than to be given a juicy nugget of information from someone who will then not go on the record. In addition to causing frustration, journalists may also view your off the record comments as suspicious, with the possibility that what you are saying is ill-informed or malicious. Where possible, everything you say should be on the record.

Key complaints from journalists

The key complaints from journalists and how to resolve them:

1. A lack of understanding about what makes a good news story or case study: Spend time getting to know a publication or broadcaster, what type of content it runs and who its audience is. Then tailor your pitch specifically to that publication or broadcaster, making sure your story and/or case study offers something new, exciting and relevant.

2. Slow and bureaucratic internal processes that result in missed deadlines: Prepare as much as possible in advance. Have case studies ready to go. Make sure all spokespeople have been media trained. Allow the PR person to have autonomy and authority.

3. The use of too much jargon that makes content boring and difficult for the lay person to understand: Don't use technical language. Use plain English. Keep it simple.

4. Trying to control the message: Work with the journalist to develop the best angle for the publication/programme, and then provide the information they need to present that angle accurately. And then let go. It will serve you better in the long run.

Copyright

Copyright can often be an area that is overlooked. Yet there are financial and legal implications associated with copying and sharing content that doesn't belong to you.

The two organisations responsible for media licensing are the Newspaper Licensing Association (NLA) and the Copyright Licensing Agency (CLA) – the former covers newspaper content while the later focuses on magazines and trade publications. Both organisations issue licences and enforce copyright regulations. If you compile coverage books or keep clippings for reference then you may need a licence.

Even if you employ a monitoring agency, you will still need a licence if you plan on doing the following things:

- Photocopying articles for storing, or passing around the office
- Storing digital copies (for up to 28 days) and distributing these among colleagues
- Emailing scanned content to contacts outside of your organisation
- Receiving hyperlinks from a licensed press cuttings agency or media monitoring organisation
- Sharing links via a secure intranet.

Copyright is also important where images are concerned. Many organisations 'borrow' images from Google to use in presentations, reports and other marketing materials without first securing permission from the owner. This can land them in trouble and at risk of hefty fines. If you're using Google Images to search for copyright photos, use the usage rights search tool to select images labelled for non-commercial reuse. Other good places to look for copyright free images are Creative Commons and pixabay.com.

It is not always the case that permission means paying out expensive fees. Photographers and designers are often willing to allow charities to use their images for free, in exchange for appropriate credits and acknowledgements.

How Centrepoint punches above its weight

Centrepoint is a youth homelessness charity. Working directly in London, Bradford and Sunderland it provides homeless 16 to 25 year-olds with a safe place to stay, but also vital support in tackling physical and mental health problems and help to return to education or find work. Here **Chris Gerrard**, the charity's PR and media manager, explains how his team approaches its media strategy.

There are just two of us in the PR team. We're responsible for all proactive and reactive communications with journalists in relation to Centrepoint and the Homeless Football Association. Responsibility for social media, internal communications, publications and direct marketing sit elsewhere but our remit is still a broad one.

A lot of our time and energy goes into maintaining our basic press office function, reacting to requests from journalists and giving them access to the information, places and most importantly the people they need, because the relationships we build as a result are crucial when we come to proactively promote our work. If we've helped a journalist in the past we find it far easier to grab their attention with our story ideas at a later date.

We focus on always being contactable, quick to respond and as helpful as possible, so one of us is always on call for media inquiries out of hours, with one of our senior spokespeople on standby. We need to be mindful of time and resources, so having a pre-agreed stance on key issues (eg rough sleeping, the housing crisis, youth unemployment) helps whoever is on duty to quickly give journalists an initial understanding of our position on a particular topic. It's not possible to anticipate all lines of inquiry but setting aside regular time with our policy and public affairs colleagues to discuss the messages we want to convey has really helped, making us a better resource for journalists and setting boundaries on which issues we will and won't comment on.

We don't issue a statement on something unless we have a clear opinion to offer. We're never provocative for the sake of it, but we've learned there's little value in sitting on the fence, your voice simply doesn't cut through. So before we issue something we always try to ask ourselves: is this meaningful and interesting for the audience, does it add something useful to the debate? If the answer to either of those is no, then our time is best spent elsewhere.

Our time is planned out roughly in 12-week periods but unless a news hook is time-dependent, such as an event, I'm not in favour of setting arbitrary deadlines. Too many charities seemingly release interesting new research without having prepared beneficiaries or other case studies to add a human dimension to their findings. It's not easy, particularly if those the charity works with are vulnerable, and is often time consuming, but it can be done and we've found it not only opens up more potential platforms for coverage such as broadcast media, but that the messages communicated are often more powerful coming from those directly affected by an issue.

When we're briefed to work on a project by colleagues we start by asking them what they want to achieve, what they're doing, when, where, why and with whom. It may be that PR isn't the best channel through which to solve their problem, or that there simply isn't a news hook. Charities can be a bit prone to navel-gazing: just because the work is really valuable doesn't make it a news story. After all, journalists expect charities to be helping in some way: it's why we exist. Reminding colleagues of that can sometimes be difficult but having an honest conversation to set expectations at an early stage is really important. Persistently pitching ideas with no news value to a journalist is likely to damage a relationship.

In our experience exclusivity of approach to journalists is becoming increasingly important. We don't have a general press list or send releases out en masse – instead we often work with small numbers of journalists on a particular story, perhaps providing one a news piece, another a case-study-led feature shortly thereafter, another a blog analysing the issue in a wider context. We still report outputs like the number of pieces we've generated, but we also monitor whether the messages we want to communicate are being used and, where we can, what happened as a result. Measuring impact doesn't have to be complicated – it could be tracking if you're getting more phone calls about your event, contacts from MPs, more volunteering offers – but it's important to know how your work is contributing to the charity's overall goals.[9]

[9] For more information visit www.centrepoint.org.uk

Chapter 6 in a nutshell

- Follow house style, avoid using jargon and be mindful of copyright issues, deadlines, and publication schedules.
- Follow the brief – to the letter. There is nothing more frustrating than contributors who think they know better than the journalist or editor.
- The story belongs to the journalist or editor, not you. You cannot control the message. Being overly protective of the message is only going to serve to irritate them and ruin your chances of securing coverage. Work with the journalist to help them develop the best angle, and then provide them with the information they need to present that angle accurately.

7
LAYING THE GROUNDWORK

In Chapter 8, we will discuss crisis communications and how to handle negative stories. However, before we go into that, there are a number of ways in which charity PR people can work either to avoid a crisis in the first place, or to help cushion the blow when the proverbial hits the fan.

Positive coverage of your work and the difference it makes

Investing in a proactive media strategy that helps secure positive coverage of your work and the difference it makes doesn't just serve to increase donations. It can also provide a softer landing if and when a negative story occurs – a strong reputation can help fend off accusations from journalists, and minimise the impact on public trust and confidence.

Good relationships with key players

Investing time in building relationships with key internal and external players can reap rewards during a crisis. By doing this you will have already built trust and confidence, and you will have (hopefully) willing allies who are prepared to stand up and defend you. The use of advocates during a crisis can add weight to your argument and help (re)build your credibility.

Public understanding of how your charity operates

Many of the 'shocking' revelations within the tabloid press about salaries, admin costs and fundraising techniques stem from a lack of understanding about how charities operate in the modern world. It is every charity's responsibility to address these issues at every given opportunity. It is your job to normalise what you do, and to remove all elements of shock and surprise. This could include the following:

- Within stories of your work, mention how the services were paid for thanks to the contributions from donors, referencing specific fundraising techniques where appropriate and relevant. Such as: "The money to pay for this service was raised via our face-to-face fundraisers in Birmingham"; or "This service was funded thanks to the generosity of all those who donated to our Christmas fundraising appeal."
- Invite journalists in to see your organisation at work, taking time to

explain about running costs, the specialist skills needed and the cost of recruiting these professionals etc.
- Providing information to supporters (donors and volunteers) via newsletters, your website, social media, and other communications, that explains how much it costs to run your organisation, the role the chief executive plays etc.

Myton Hospice – CEO's salaries blog

In September 2015 Myton Hospice was the subject of negative media coverage by *The Times* about its team's salaries. Its then chief executive **Kate Lee** wrote a blog in response, focusing on the information the journalists had chosen to ignore. Excerpts from this blog provide an example of the type of background information all charities should be sharing about their operations and the roles and responsibilities of their teams.

My director of income generation has a target of 117 times her salary – yep, I typed it right 117 times. What does she get if she achieves it? Nothing, no bonuses or commission paid here. What does she get if she doesn't achieve it? The pain of seeing services cut and a gut-wrenching guilt that somehow, she is personally to blame…

My director of finance has the responsibility for ensuring every single penny we spend on non-salaries at Myton is spent wisely. That is about £3.5m spent over some 30,000 transactions. This financial year she has already saved over £100,000 and just yesterday she was successful in getting a revaluation of our VAT, saving us a further £25,000. She is technically excellent, highly skilled and very persuasive and pretty much pays her own way through the saving she haggles.

My director of strategy spends time liaising with the NHS to ensure we work together as collaboratively as possible... His time is spent ensuring that the NHS considers our far more cost-effective and significantly higher-quality options for care when they go through their numerous change initiatives. In the last four months he has negotiated a £200,000 contribution to six new palliative care beds for Coventry hospice: as a result we will be able to support up to 72 additional patients next year. Again, we need to attract and employ staff that understand the NHS commissioning but are prepared to earn about 20% less than they would if they just worked for the NHS.

The director of nursing...ours runs an organisation that has a 98% patient and family satisfaction rate. They have to retain nurses in a national nurse shortage, in a small organisation with limited career development opportunities. They deliver inpatient and community based care, they manage over 15 other specialisms, from chaplains to art therapists. They manage increasing demand, increasing complexity and the pain of not being able to meet everyone's needs, with a team of nursing staff working at the very cutting edge of psychologically demanding work. It is more than just necessary that every single patient has an outstanding experience at Myton because they deserve and require it. Our entire voluntary income is based on our reputation as an amazing provider of end of life care – getting it wrong with just one family could have a devastating effect on the entire operation...

Kate then goes on to close her blog with the following statement...

We don't want to remain a sticking plaster for people who have nowhere else to turn; we want to solve their problems once and for all. I want every single person in Coventry and Warwickshire to live well and have a good, natural death, the way they want it to be with their loved ones supported, but I must attract the best and brightest if I have a cat in hell's chance of achieving it...

Internal understanding of how the media operates

Even the most highly skilled communications professionals can fail to respond effectively to a crisis if there are difficulties internally. Information cover-ups and leaks, a lack of understanding of PR and journalists' needs, delays and lack of appreciation for deadlines can all hinder a response. Identifying where this type of challenge may lie, and putting measures in place to address them early – such as sending all relevant people on media training and by nurturing key relationships – can be a useful exercise.

Media training and interviewing techniques

The interview. That all important 'conversation' with a journalist, from which they will turn in a story that will could either benefit you or harm your organisation. From the two-minute interrogation on live radio, to the 'chat' by the bar at that conference, to the longer telephone interview, your response to a journalist's questions could make or break you.

Given that some people define news as the publication or broadcast of information that others don't want you to see or hear, it goes without saying that not all interviews go smoothly. Even if the interview is to be about a positive topic, it's important to remember that the journalist has an agenda and is likely to challenge your view points. As such interviews can be a source of tension.

With this in mind, it's important that the people you put forward for interviews are not only properly briefed but can hold their own. In times of crisis, in particular, it is vitally important to ensure that your spokesperson is media trained (there are lots of places out there that offer training in this area – see Useful resources, page 110) and can cope with being under intense pressure. To offer someone to the media who may be out of their comfort zone could end up doing more damage than good. If there is no one internally who can respond during a crisis then putting forward a credible third party who can vouch for you could be a suitable alternative.

Your spokesperson needs to be an eloquent and engaging speaker, who can talk in language that everyone can understand, not just those who work in their particular field. Journalists are looking for interviewees who can properly explain what they mean – one word answers or responses full of jargon simply will not do.

Ensuring your spokesperson is briefed – even if they are an expert on the subject at hand – is paramount for an effective interview. They should know your organisation's 'line' and ideally have three key messages (see Chapter 3) that they absolutely need to get across. They should be able to weave them into the conversation, even if the journalist's questions are threatening to take them in a different direction. Bridging techniques to divert the interview back to where they want it to be can help here. For example: 'That's an important point, but it's also important to remember that...' or 'I don't know the answer to that specifically but what I do know is this...'

Take some time to research the journalist and their publication or show beforehand as this can give clues as to what their agenda may be and the tone that they may take. And remember that although journalists can ask seemingly stupid questions, this feigned ignorance tends to be a technique by which they can source soundbites and specific quotes that serve to explain the issue at hand.

If this is a crisis comms interview then the interviewee needs to be prepared for a real grilling. It is important to be transparent but the speaker also needs to make sure that what they say and how they say it isn't going to be misconstrued or twisted out of context. A crib sheet featuring bullet points and key messages can help, unless it is a television interview, in which case it would be visible and therefore inappropriate.

Phone interviews can often be the easiest to do. Notes can be kept close at hand and others can listen in or record the conversation. However, remember that it is more difficult to build up rapport when on the phone as the journalist can't see your winning smile or the fact that you're nodding in agreement.

Face-to-face interviews, particularly those for written features, tend to be a longer, possibly more relaxed experience than a news interview which is hurried and often live. Feature writers will also include information on the character and circumstance of their interviewee and will include detail of what they see around them, so if you're fidgeting, sweating and looking nervous you're not going to come across well in the final piece. Make sure you wear appropriate clothing and are seated comfortably. You will perform best if you try to relax and be yourself. This same sentiment applies for television interviews.

Interview tips

- Speak clearly and calmly (even if the interview is challenging).
- Don't use jargon.
- Don't waffle, but don't use one word answers either.
- Try and get your key messages out when answering the questions.
- If you don't know the answer, say so. Don't lie and get it wrong.
- If on television or in a face-to-face interview, don't fidget.
- Relax – you will perform better.

Lack of clear and detailed note-taking/records

It is absolutely essential that all the information you provide either to the media or other key stakeholders is accurate. Poor internal processes and record-keeping throughout your organisation can hinder this. As too can those people who may have made mistakes and are now fearful that they are going to be blamed, who may even hide or doctor information. For example, the *Daily Mail* contacts you to say they are running a story about your organisation having hired people who are registered sex offenders. You will need to check your internal records to establish if this is true or not. If it is false, you will need to demonstrate this is the case.

Equally, it is important to keep accurate records during a crisis communication situation. Do not rely on memory alone to get you through. If your crisis escalates and you end up in court in a year or even two, not having written notes to refer to could make it difficult for you to defend your reputation.

Poor record keeping can also result in missed opportunities. For instance, a journalist wants to run a story on the generosity of the residents of Derby. You know you have lots of donors in this area but your database is incomplete and disorganised. By the time you've collated the data, the moment has passed.

Chapter 7 in a nutshell

- Investing in a proactive media strategy that helps to secure positive coverage of your work and the difference it makes can provide a softer landing if and when a negative story occurs, helping to protect your reputation.
- Investing time in building relationships with key internal and external players can reap rewards during a crisis. By doing this you will have already built trust and confidence, and you will have (hopefully) willing allies who are prepared to stand up and defend you.
- Media training and effective internal systems and processes can make the difference between a strong and credible reputation, and one that is neither of those.
- Your response to a journalist's questions could make or break you. Even if the interview is to be about a positive topic, remember the journalist has an agenda and is likely to challenge your view points. As such interviews can be a source of tension and should be rehearsed and prepared for.

8
DEALING WITH NEGATIVE STORIES

Once upon a time, public trust in charities was so high they rarely received any negative coverage at all – it was implicit in their charitable status that they were saintly organisations that never put a foot wrong.

Those days are no longer with us. Charities are now under the media microscope like never before. This, combined with the chasm between public perceptions of how charities operate and the realities, means we are seeing more and more stories that claim charities are being mismanaged, wasteful and using less than ethical practices.

It is not just stories about charity operations that can create a crisis. Stories about events happening elsewhere, which relate to a charity's work, can also require charity PR people to deliver effective reactive communications that negate any associated risks and capitalise on opportunities. For instance, dodgy behaviour by a celebrity patron or a high profile death caused by an illness that relates to your work could require your PR person to go into overdrive. Handle these badly and it could have devastating impact upon your organisation's greatest asset – its reputation.

This chapter provides an overview of how to identify, prepare for and react to a media crisis. For more detailed information, visit www.charitycomms.org.uk or read the *Guardian* Voluntary Sector Network's risk guides, published in associated with Zurich – both of which are useful sources of information on this topic. It would also be a valuable exercise to invest in crisis comms training (see Chapter 7).

What is a crisis?

In times of intense difficulty, or when important decisions need to be made, others may lose their head. It's important you don't lose yours.

Sometimes a crisis can appear quickly and unexpectedly, such as a death, natural disaster or accident, or an unguarded comment made on social media or to a journalist. Sometimes they can develop gradually – the result of a prolonged period of financial difficulties, poor recruitment practices or changes in government policy. Many are predictable. Others are caused by the deliberate actions of those within your organisation. Not all of these will pose an immediate threat to your organisation, but the way you respond to it could.

Preparation is the most effective way to prevent a crisis or to stop it from escalating in the event one occurs. Those charities that don't have a crisis management plan should write one. This should see trustees, the chief executive, programmes teams and those responsible for fundraising, PR and communications getting together to brainstorm the potential risks and the impact they could have on the business. From the death of a beneficiary in your care, to a member of staff or volunteer acting inappropriately to accusations of mismanagement and fraud, there are any number of crises that could result in negative media coverage, and subsequently a loss of funding, damaged reputation and, worst case scenario, services or even the entire organisation having to close down.

How to prevent a crisis (or respond if one occurs)

In a crisis, time is of the essence and all action needs to be swift, decisive and appropriate. This means having protocols in place that outline step-by-step instructions regarding who needs to be informed, when and about what; the role each individual must play, and what information must be easily available to defuse the situation. It may be helpful to break this down by the different stages of the crisis, such as immediate tasks, the first 24-72 hours, post-crisis etc. Having all of this prepared in advance will save a great deal of much needed time if and when disaster does hit.

Addressing problems quickly, before they get out of hand, is essential. One way to do this is to create an alert system so that anyone who comes across anything they think might be a risk or a potential problem knows who to talk to and pass messages on. But be realistic. The comms person doesn't want to be informed every time the charity receives a minor complaint, but it might be helpful to receive a monthly round-up of complaints, which could give away clues as to problems that are brewing in the background.

Free and paid-for tools, such as Google Alerts, Hootsuite, Gorkana and PR Newswire, should be used to monitor coverage and alert you to any stories mentioning your name and that need to be followed up immediately.

Making sure the chief executive has been media trained is a must. They and other key stakeholders will need to be confident spokespeople in front of journalists. In times of crisis, when emotions are running high, this role will be made all the harder if they have no experience of media interviews (see Chapter 7).

Clearly, the media doesn't need to know about all the crises your organisation is dealing with – and indeed part of the role of a good PR is to keep bad news out of the press. However, if you are facing a particular issue that you feel is likely to make its way into the media, then it can be in your interest to approach journalists with the information yourself, before the story is leaked by someone else, as this way you control the message rather than the message controlling you.

However, if a journalist is knocking at your door, or a negative story has already hit the headlines, you need to respond quickly, calmly and accurately. This can be difficult if you don't have the full facts available to you, which is where a holding statement can be handy. These can be drafted in advance – based upon the risks you have previously identified or being a simple generic line, such as: "We are investigating the situation and will be making more information available as soon as we can."

Whatever you say, do not, under any circumstances, say "no comment". This statement is laden with suspicion and to use it implies that you have something to hide, which could make the situation worse. If you don't know the answer to a journalist's question then say you will get back to them with an answer. Check their deadline, confirm the question and then go away and investigate – making sure that you do indeed meet the deadline. Ignoring it won't make it go away.

Make sure that everyone within the organisation knows who is authorised to speak to the media. The last thing you want is a member of staff who has not been briefed telling a journalist something they shouldn't have.

You need to work as fast as possible to find out all the facts. You will need to ask questions, such as what happened and when, who is responsible, have we done something wrong and need to apologise or can we defend our position, will admitting responsibility have legal or financial repercussions, do we need to take action and does this story have the potential to be on-going or can we put the fire out?

As Damien McBride wrote in the *Guardian* in September 2015, during times of crisis, there was one essential question that all PR professionals must ask of the person at the heart of whatever story has got the media into a spin: "'What's the truth?' Not, 'What shall we say?' or, 'How do you want me to handle it?' but instead the absolute insistence on knowing the full, unvarnished facts before deciding whether and how to spin them."[10]

There is a lot to be said for the phrase "honesty is the best policy". The truth will out eventually and lies will only come back to haunt you, which will make the situation much worse and possibly do irreparable damage to your brand and its reputation.

---

10 From *How do you deal with a story like #piggate? A spindoctor's view.*

Stick to the facts. Don't deliberately miss out certain information if it doesn't work in your favour as this can be damaging. Certainly don't speculate, and avoid adding any opinion. This can be difficult if you are upset, worried or angry.

Demonstrate that you are working to address or investigate the issue. If necessary, explain how you are doing this, either by conducting an investigation, speaking to relevant stakeholders, putting a service on hold, working with independent auditors etc. Show you are concerned, but try not to over-commit to something you ultimately won't be able to deliver. Keep people at the forefront. Empathise with those affected; consider your beneficiaries and supporters, then your staff.

If there are genuinely extenuating circumstances or contexts don't be afraid to mention them. It may be important for people to understand that you have had to end provision of a particular service because of government cuts; or to know that outsourcing fundraising was a more cost-efficient way for you to generate valuable funds than if you did it in-house.

It is really important to recognise that all of this has to happen immediately. If a key member of the crisis response team is in a meeting, pull them out of it. If someone is on holiday, Skype them in. If they are unavailable, then hold the meeting without them. A crisis won't wait until it's convenient for you to respond to it. It is happening now and therefore needs to be dealt with now. It takes a matter of seconds for a tweet to travel around the world. Imagine how much damage could be being caused while your team mulls over its response.

Suggested statements

1. Story: High levels of pay for the chief executive or senior staff

Response: A charity's board is responsible for setting the salaries of its senior management team and so should be willing to defend them. Therefore a statement from the chair or a trustee has a big role to play here. Ideally the statement will explain how the role of chief executive is highly complex and requires a skilled, qualified individual at the helm. Detail about what is involved in the role can be helpful. This might include details of the scope of the charity's work (be that negotiating difficult routes through areas of conflict or understanding complex laboratory experiments to ensure the best medical research projects are selected), the size of the team being managed, and the need to ensure that the millions donated by the public and received as part of government contracts are well managed and well spent. See this excellent explanation in the *Guardian* from Mencap CEO Jan Tregelles on the reality of being a salary CEO and why they deserve their pay: http://www.theguardian.com/voluntary-sector-network/2013/nov/11/mencap-chief-executive-defends-salary

2. Story: Aggressive fundraising practices
Response: All fundraising charities should abide by the Institute of Fundraising's Code of Fundraising Practice. If you find that you have not abided by the code then admit it, apologise and demonstrate how you will bring about the necessary changes. If you have stuck to the code, explain that is the case. Fundraisers should never be ashamed of their role, or for being paid to do it. Emphasise how charities have a duty to both the donor and to the beneficiary and that it is the fundraisers' job to balance those duties. This means asking the public for support, but asking them well. Referencing research that shows how people do not give without being asked can help.

3. Story: High admin costs, which are deemed to be wasteful
Response: Charities should do what they can to spend money carefully and to avoid waste. However, it is impossible for a charity to be well-run and deliver impact without having some operating costs. This should be explained to the media in response to any such stories, providing evidence as to the value effective administration offers, be it more highly skilled staff, a warm, safe space for your frontline workers or indeed the most basic of requirements – that your electricity bills are paid so you can keep your lights on. Jeremy Hughes, CEO of the Alzheimer's Society, robustly tackles the myths around charity pay and admin spending for the *Guardian*: http://www.theguardian.com/voluntary-sector-network/2015/jul/14/myths-charity-pay-staff-income-sun-alzheimers-society

Other stakeholder communications

In times of crisis it isn't just the media which needs to be updated. Staff and volunteers, and key stakeholders such as patrons, donors/funders and delivery partners also need to be kept in the loop.

A lack of communication is a surefire way to build mistrust, suspicion and rumour. Instead focus on reliable, transparent and regular updates across your website, newsletters, social media and direct emails, which will ensure all relevant stakeholders feel valued and confident in the organisation's response.

Patrons, large funders and delivery partners can also be useful allies, and depending on the crisis, may be willing to go on the record in support of your work. This can help add weight and credibility to your response and may help defuse whatever negativity abounds.

Once the heat is off

When the crisis is over, it's important to review what happened and how you responded. Establishing which sections of the media plan worked or worked better than others, whether everyone responded in the way they were supposed to and whether there were unforeseen consequences will be helpful in allowing you to update the plan and make it better.

Included within this evaluation should be an assessment of your brand reputation, donation levels and credibility within key circles. Not only will this allow you to focus your follow-up communications on the most urgent and important areas but it will also provide data that can be used within a business case for increased investment in the PR team.

Don't forget to look for positives as well as negatives. It is very easy to say that the PR person should look for opportunities during a disaster, but when the heat is on and your reputation has been damaged it can be difficult to find anything positive to focus on. However, there can be potential upsides to a crisis that shouldn't be over looked – such as a raised profile for your organisation, the cause and your chief executive – and should be capitalised on as much as possible via your follow-up communications strategy.

The Trussell Trust takes a stand against negative reporting

In April 2015, the Trussell Trust found itself at the centre of a media storm regarding its statistics on foodbank usage. **Emma Thorogood**, assistant press officer at the charity, explains how they handled the situation.

The Trussell Trust has always sought to speak out on hunger in the UK. One of our key roles as a media team is to debunk the increasingly pervasive stereotypes and myths about the 'undeserving poor', and to explain why food poverty is a problem in the UK today. One of the important ways we do this is to empower people who have been referred to foodbanks to share their experiences, raising awareness of what hunger feels like and challenging the narratives pushed by programmes like 'Benefits Britain' and 'Benefits Street'. Trussell Trust foodbank statistics, which show the number of three day emergency food supplies provided by our national network of over 400 foodbanks, give us a unique opportunity to reinforce real stories with national figures that highlight the scale of the problem.

What we've found out over the years is that speaking out on the reality of hunger and poverty does not always make you popular, and as a team we have to be ready for a negative backlash. Putting our head above the parapet has historically led to attempts to undermine The Trussell Trust's credibility, and this is always heightened when we publish our annual financial year data on foodbank use every April. Never before was this as apparent as during our last press release on foodbank use, published in April 2015 against the backdrop of a general election. The Trussell Trust trustees made a decision to go ahead with publishing our figures at the same time as we do every year, maintaining consistency of reporting.

Just ahead of publication of the figures, a major national newspaper ran an article actively trying to discredit The Trussell Trust. Following our press release, there were over 3,000 media hits relating to The Trussell Trust and/or foodbanks that week, and phones were ringing off the hook as broadcasters and newspapers sought comment. Much of the coverage shone an important spotlight on UK hunger, but it did not secure only positive coverage. During the week of the release we were questioned about the reliability of our figures, and how they were articulated. In each of these instances, the Trussell Trust's robust media strategy worked quickly and effectively both in and out of hours to handle difficult situations.

Once statements had been formulated in response to a crisis/ negative media, we acted quickly to circulate these internally, and then disseminate them externally. We firmly rebutted and clarified various misleading pieces, and shared our clarification statement on Twitter with users who had been tweeting incorrect information. This actually led to some apologies from people who had tweeted misleading articles.

Our media team consists of three full-time members of staff, but we are also extremely fortunate to be supported by people within our senior management team, regional teams and our board of trustees, who understand the importance of engaging with the media and of dealing with crises as quickly as possible. Members of our senior team are media trained to give interviews and respond to difficult questions under pressure – an invaluable attribute during this period, which kept a clear message on our statistics in the public eye.

Our Head of Media, Molly Hodson, had a lengthy discussion with Patrick Butler, the society editor at the *Guardian*, and he consequently wrote one of the most informed pieces we have seen about Trussell Trust data: http://www.theguardian.com/society/patrick-butler-cuts-blog/2015/may/04/those-food-bank-data-complicated-yes-exaggerated-no

Whilst we faced much greater challenges around the release of our figures in 2015 than in previous years, there was much more positive coverage than negative, and there is no doubt that the problem of food poverty and hunger in the UK was yet again raised as a key issue that our nation must face.

Chapter 8 in a nutshell

- Plan, plan and plan some more. Preparation is essential if PR crises are to be handled effectively.
- Crisis response has to happen immediately. A crisis won't wait until it's convenient for you to respond to it. It is happening now and therefore needs to be dealt with now.
- Don't be afraid to apologise if need be, or defend yourself if you haven't done anything wrong. Make sure everything you say is 100% accurate and cannot be misconstrued.
- Under no circumstances, should you ever say "no comment", which only serves to create suspicion and mistrust.
- A lack of communication is a surefire way to build mistrust, suspicion and rumour. Instead focus on reliable, transparent and regular updates across your website, newsletters, social media and direct emails, which will ensure all relevant stakeholders feel valued and confident in the organisation's response.

9
SOCIAL MEDIA

All good PR strategies will incorporate the use of social media channels, such as Twitter, Facebook, LinkedIn and others.

Why is the use of social media important for media relations? There are three main reasons:

1. Journalists look to social media for content.
2. It enables you to reach non-traditional media influencers, such as social producers and bloggers.
3. It allows you to tell your story in your own words.

Social media as a source of content

Journalists frequently look to social media channels, such as Twitter and Facebook, for story ideas, case studies, potential interviewees – and importantly to gauge the mood around a particular topic. By using your social media feeds to share success stories and press releases, demonstrate your authority and to build your reputation in a key field, it can help you become the go-to person for comments and contributions.

Journalists also put out requests across social media when they are looking for case studies and expert opinion. Keep your eye out for the hashtag #journorequest or #prrequest as these may send opportunities your way.

And as mentioned in Chapter 2, contacting journalists directly, either by sending them information straight to their Twitter handle or by responding to one of their own tweets, can help build that relationship further.

Given there are thousands of social media channels in existence and hundreds more popping up all the time, it is important to remain focused and only use those that are going to add most value. I would recommend concentrating on the following:

Twitter: Used by charities, businesses, individuals, journalists and other key influencers to share information about their work and that of others. Not only is it a great way to stay on top of current conversations and trends, but it can help you strengthen awareness and understanding of your cause.

Facebook: Using Facebook as an online PR tool allows organisations to increase their reach exponentially when content is shared and reshared. That content could be latest news, case studies, new statistics etc.

LinkedIn: This professional networking website can support your PR efforts in a number of ways, including researching journalists before pitching to them, facilitating introductions to key journalists, editors and bloggers, gathering intelligence on your market, audience and competitors, and reaching new audiences.

YouTube: YouTube should not be overlooked as a PR tool. It should be used as a free distribution channel for your videos and television adverts (if you are lucky enough to have such a thing), and you can use tools such as Google Hangouts to create online events, debates and discussions that are then published automatically on YouTube, that journalists can be invited to participate in or view.

Extending your reach

Did you know that the lifestyle blogger Zoella has now had more than 11 million page views on her YouTube channel, or that Ewdison Then is the highest-earning blogger in the world and rakes in around $70,000 a month from his posts? PR strategies today should incorporate non-traditional media – and in order to reach these people you need to be where they are.

Add to this the potential that social sharing offers – when individuals share stories to their own networks – and suddenly there is a much wider audience available to you, one that can keep a story running for much longer than it usually would.

The same rules apply when targeting bloggers as they do to other journalists and media outlets – content needs to be appropriate for the audience, relevant, interesting and new. However, if you want your story to be spread far and wide by other people, then it also needs to be shareable.

How to create shareable, viral content goes beyond the reach of this guide, but suggestions include the use of infographics, video and lists (everyone loves a list – hence Buzzfeed becoming so popular on the back of its 'listicles'), and creating a fun initiative for people to participate in. Check out the Useful Resources section at the back of this guide for links to more information and inspiration on this area.

Your story in your words

As we have discussed earlier in this guide, by handing over a story to a journalist, you lose control of it. Social media offers the opportunity for you to publish the bits the journalist has missed, to add extra detail, correct any misconceptions and to direct people to where they can find more information on your website. And it does this quickly– far quicker than waiting for a press release to do the rounds.

This can be particularly important during times of crisis. If you know a story is about to hit the press and is going to be less than favourable, you can utilise social media to explain the situation from your point of view before anyone else gets there first. In some cases, this may even kill the story before it runs. You can also use it to correct misconceptions and errors that other people may have made about your work.

Social media in a crisis

For every opportunity social media offers there are accompanying risks: the lack of control, a negative comment spreading like wildfire, the limits of 140 characters... A crisis might start on social media or it may spread on social media. Either way, you need to consider how you will respond.

See Chapter 8 for more information on how to handle a crisis. However, I would add that it is important to remember that everything you say on Twitter and some other social media channels is public. Therefore, you must apply the same legal advice to social media outputs as you would to any other statements and be careful what you tweet. A good rule of thumb is never to tweet something you wouldn't say to someone's face or that you wouldn't be happy about your grandma or boss seeing. Never tweet in anger and certainly not when drunk!

Finally don't forget to respond to complaints. This means constant monitoring, including evenings and weekends, to ensure you don't miss a disgruntled supporter or service user. The best thing to do is to get the complaint off social media – give them a named personal email address to contact and get back to them as soon as you can.

Using social media to build a relationship with a local newspaper journalist

Amber Valley Angels' communications officer identified a journalist on a well-read local paper she thought could be a key contact for the charity. She initially searched for the journalist on Twitter and followed her. She then made a note of the type of stories the journalist liked to cover and the type of issues she would tweet about. If any of the journalist's posts were relevant to the work of Amber Valley Angels, the comms officer would retweet them.

When the charity had something interesting to say, either via its website or a press release, the comms officer would tweet links out, including directly to the journalist. For instance, "Local older people in Amber Valley have been abandoned by relatives who've moved away. For more visit bit.ly/24bC5i9 @journoname".

If the journalist asked questions or was looking for specific information relevant to Amber Valley Angels, the comms officer would provide an answer or direction to the appropriate resource. This often involved providing case studies for features and news stories.

This activity culminated in Amber Valley Angels offering the journalist an exclusive on its new research into the council's budget cuts and the impact on local people. A direct message was sent to the journalist who agreed to meet in person to discuss the story in more detail. The end result was a front-page headline story and a double-page special report in the centre of the newspaper.

As a follow-on to this story, the journalist then agreed to chair a Google Hangout for Amber Valley Angels that brought together speakers from community organisations and the local council to discuss the key issues facing older people in the area. The event was advertised in the local newspaper and via social media. It was broadcast live and then a link posted on YouTube for participants and viewers to share and use after the event. The event was watched by people all over the country, and the chief executive of Amber Valley Angels subsequently invited to Westminster to attend a parliamentary event on ageing.

Chapter 9 in a nutshell

- Use social media to share success stories and press releases, demonstrate your authority and to build your reputation in a key field to help you become the go-to person for comments and contributions.
- Keep your eye out for journalist requests, in particular via the hashtag #journorequest or #prrequest as these may send opportunities your way.
- Contacting journalists directly, either by sending them information straight to their Twitter handle or by responding to one of their own tweets, can help build relationships with key media contacts.

10
MONITORING AND EVALUATION

What does success look like? This is an important question to ask, both of your PR person and others in relevant departments. It is very important to be realistic about what you can achieve, to manage the expectations of others and so you can build a case for further investment should you want it.

I regularly have conversations with colleagues who work within PR about clients who have expected us to deliver them the front page of the *Financial Times* or a slot on Newsnight, when that simply wasn't going to happen as, frankly, their stories just weren't that interesting.

The level of coverage you achieve is almost entirely dependent upon the relevance and strength of the stories you produce. Therefore, if you have weak case studies, a lack of data and/or evidence-based opinion, and a limited selection of well-composed, high-resolution photography, the mainstream press is automatically going to be out of reach for you.

You should also be careful not to be too ambitious with regards to the volume of coverage you can achieve. Journalists and their stories can be demanding. If you work alone in comms or are part of a small team, you may find you become overwhelmed with the number of requests and speed at which they need to be fulfilled – which could have a damaging impact upon your reputation.

Benchmarking

You can only begin to assess how successful you have been, if you first understand where you started. Therefore, the first step in monitoring and evaluation is to establish what you want to measure and the baseline against which all future activity will be benchmarked.

Once you have established your baseline, you can then determine targets that you want to reach.

It may be that you want to improve a certain demographic's awareness of you so they use your services more, you may want to promote a fundraising appeal or event, or you may want to instigate behavior or policy change. Your end goals will determine what you need to benchmark.

Useful things to benchmark before you begin are:

- Current levels of media coverage
- Website traffic
- Social media engagement (likes, followers, shares etc)

- Donation levels
- Volunteer enquiries
- Number of people using a service
- Volume of event participants
- Number of signatures on a petition
- The nature of what people say about you, be that positive, negative or indifferent
- Your competitors and their media coverage (can you learn from them, measure yourself against or differentiate yourself from them?)
- Levels of brand recognition

This process can be as extensive or as light touch as you see fit, depending on your resources and how much time you have. You may simply wish to set up a spreadsheet in which to record basic data, or you could conduct detailed brand analysis via a specialist agency.

How to monitor results (volume v value)

The *volume* of press activity is relatively easy to track. In addition to tracking the email and phone requests received from journalists, there are many tools available that will help you keep count of the coverage that features your name but where a journalist didn't contact you directly.

Some of these tools are free. For example, Google Alert allows you to see every time a new piece of content mentioning your name is published on the internet. Alternatively you can pay for a media monitoring and press clipping service. Companies in this space include PR Newswire, Gorkana, Cision, Precise and Meltwater.

Digital traffic can be monitored in a number of ways. Google Analytics provides very useful insight into your own website, how people find you, what they look at and how long they stay on particular pages, among other things. Alexa.com and Comscore offer traffic metrics from across the web that can help build competitive intelligence and strategic insight.

For social media, there is a wealth of free and paid-for tools available, such as Klout, which provides an indication as to the breadth of your influence to Followerwonk, which provides information as to who is following you, where they live and when they are most engaged. Hootsuite's search functionality allows you to monitor particular hashtags and phrases that people are using on social media, as well as your own Twitter handle.

Understanding the value of media coverage is more difficult. We all know someone who thinks a piece in print is more influential than a piece on *Mail Online* and would never be convinced that the right blogger could have more influence than either. So how can you measure what PR is worth?

Many years ago, PR professionals would sit with a ruler and a bundle of newspapers and literally measure the size of 'column inches'. They would then use that information to measure the advertising value equivalent (AVE) of that space. While the method of assessing AVE has changed, many people still like to use it as a means by which to compare PR activity to the purchase of advertising – not least because it tends to make the PR person or team look good when they can say they secured £1m worth of PR coverage with a budget of just £5,000, something that can be particularly helpful when justifying PR to people who only understand numbers.

However, AVE cannot capture PR outcomes (such as changed behaviour or the securing of a meeting with a government minister), cannot distinguish between the tone or style of content and the relevance of that to the PR objectives, and it can't measure the value of social shares that an article or piece of content might experience. Nor can it measure the value of keeping a client out of the media spotlight. PR is not the same as advertising and therefore shouldn't be measured in the same way.

Instead, many PRs prefer to use their own criteria to determine the value and success of a campaign or piece of content. These often include the following:

Reach: How many people were exposed to the coverage?

Relevancy: Did the audience comprise the right people, and did they receive the right messages?

Frequency: How many times will the average person have seen the coverage? Did they have repeated exposure? (Media planners tend to aim to reach priority audiences eight or nine times to achieve optimum engagement).

Comprehension: Did the target audience understand the messages? Do they now know something they didn't previously?

Context: When and where did the target audience experience or encounter the media activity? Will that impact upon their frame of mind? For instance, someone quickly flicking through a website while on the bus will engage differently to those people reading an in-depth piece while at their desk or while relaxing at home.

Attitude: What should the target audience think, feel and do?

Influence: Has it changed what people think, feel and/or do?

Additional measures of success might be:

- a change in the balance of paid-for v earned v owned v shared media
- an increased share of media compared to key competitors
- the level of engagement (the length of time people spent reading or watching a piece of content)
- their relationship to the channel in question – for instance, people tend to trust the regional press more than the national press.

Responding to errors

What do you do if someone has misquoted you? Told a lie about your organisation? Or just simply got the facts wrong.

There are clearly various degrees of error. If you were misquoted, but the impact wasn't great – for example, the published quote was on message and positive for your organisation, then it can be in your best interests to ignore the mistake.

However, if the misquote or misinformation could have a negative impact on your organisation then you should deal with it – and quickly. Errors can exist on the internet for years to come, being easily shared and repeated as people reuse content, both in the immediate term and in the future.

The first action to take is to contact the reporter and (calmly and rationally) explain what has happened. If they accept they have made a mistake, then the publication will most likely apologise verbally and make the change in the digital version of the story. If the error is deemed serious enough, the media outlet may agree to do a follow-up story setting the story straight, or print a retraction – particularly if they have libelled you and are at risk of legal action.

Libel and defamation of character are the two legal challenges that most editors and publishers dread and will do their utmost to avoid, not least because of the associated financial costs. However, if a media outlet believes it stands a chance of winning the case or if it is wealthy and feels the increased revenue from the story outweighs the court costs, then it may challenge your claim. It is then up to you to decide whether you can afford to take action, and how the loss of reputation or business compares to the cost of progressing with the case. Legal Aid is not available for libel cases and taking action against a media outlet can run into many hundreds of thousands of pounds.

Making the case for investment

Your monitoring and evaluation results can be very helpful when needing to ask senior management, trustees and even donors for more investment in PR activities.

When persuading people that additional media activity is essential if you are to help the organisation achieve a positive and transformational impact, both internally and externally, there are a number of things to consider.

Impact: Is this activity likely to make a significant contribution to your organisation's aims? Would not doing it expose the organisation to unacceptable risk?

Affordability: What resources do you need to deliver this? Will it give you a good return on investment?

Integration: Does this fit with the rest of your communications strategy? Does it complement or contradict other activity? Have you got the timing right? Can you use your other communications channels (your website, leaflets, an event etc) to support this activity?

Internal needs and expectations: Those who hold the purse strings will be motivated by a range of different propositions, and the more you understand what they are, the less chance you will have of a nasty surprise when you put your investment case in front of them. Some will look at PR from a strategic point of view, others will take a tactical perspective, focusing on whether or not you can get them quoted in next weekend's *FT*.

If your pitch includes examples of the major pieces of activity you want to invest in, you will help your board understand the overall strategy better, because you will have given them a tangible illustration of what it looks like in practice. They will also be able to see where the money is going.

People don't donate to charities they've never heard of

What's the secret to getting boards and senior teams on your side when it comes to resourcing comms activity? It's not rocket science, says **Athena Lamnisos**, CEO at the Eve Appeal. You just need to explain very clearly why PR is essential in helping deliver the charity's mission.

Developing a strategic and integrated communications strategy that matches your business objectives is absolutely key. This ensures that you target the right resources in the best places and reach your audiences. It also stops you going off on tangents – which a PR, comms and media team is sometimes wont to do. It's sometimes very tempting to view any coverage as positive.

I don't think I've interacted with a board of trustees who haven't wanted more media coverage, column inches and celebrity endorsements, but that doesn't mean that is the right thing to chase. Your strategy, communications channels and tools need to be appropriate to your issue, your audiences and the key levers that will move your objectives in the right direction.

Communications need to start from the inside. If your most important internal stakeholders don't understand what you need to say and why, then they definitely won't support resources being used in this way.

What drives me to distraction in the charity sector is duplication of effort. And there's lots of it. What often drives this duplication is competition for media voice. Media mentions become a measure for effectiveness. Well they're not. Every charity, should take a long hard look at why it exists, what it specifically can achieve, change and champion that others can't, and how it can work effectively with others to communicate a stronger message and reach new audiences.

For instance, thousands of Instagram likes or twitter shares do not change policy. Photos of celebs in the glossies at your events or wearing your branded merchandise won't feed people or cure diseases. However, they can be a very useful way in which you can reach people with your messages.

There's an all too prevalent virus that often hits communications teams – Cobbler's Children Syndrome. Like the proverbial children of shoemakers who go without shoes, comms teams fall foul of this malaise and think it's all too obvious why media, PR and brand programmes are important. As such, they don't explain how these are critical tools in meeting the charity's vision.

Ultimately, that's the message to convey to your board or senior management team at annual budget setting time. Present a strategy and action plan that are deliverable, that cover all channels and tools (not just the media the boss sees while they're eating their breakfast) and that demonstrates how it supports the delivery of your overall business objectives.

Review regularly, assess the impact, reach, style and tone of each piece, and adjust your strategy accordingly. And don't forget to celebrate your successes. Make sure the rest of your organisation knows about the great work you are doing – and of course, share it across social media as well. It all counts towards increasing your brand recognition, strengthening your reputation, and improving awareness of your cause.

Chapter 10 in a nutshell

- Understand what success looks like for you and establish a baseline against which to benchmark your activities
- Make the most of the free and paid-for tools to help you monitor coverage, such as Google Analytics, Google Alerts, PR Newswire, Klout and Followerwonk
- Help others across your organisation to understand how your media relations activities are supporting the delivery of your overall charitable objectives
- Manage expectations of what you can achieve with the resources to hand, and develop a strong business case for why media relations matter to your organisation.

11
KEY CHALLENGES FACED BY CHARITIES

CharityComms and Slack Communications surveyed 125 charities in January 2016 to identify the key challenges they face in securing media coverage. We've listed them here with reference to areas in the book where we hope you can find suggested solutions.

1. Lack of resource: we don't have enough comms staff/I don't have enough time: see pages 7, 26, 82
2. Journalists aren't interested in my stories: see pages 10-12 and 19-29
3. Journalists only want negative stories, not positive news: see pages 34-42
4. I don't have access to good case studies: see pages 35-37
5. I don't know who to contact to get press coverage: see pages 10-18
6. We don't have enough willing/confident spokespeople: see pages 82-84
7. I don't have the data to back up my stories: see pages 46-49
8. My organisation is nervous of getting negative coverage: see pages 87-95
9. I don't have access to a good camera or quality images: see pages 49-50
10. 'Sign-off' takes too long (we often miss a deadline as I wait for a response from management): see pages 72 and 82
11. I don't know how to evaluate our coverage: see pages 101-104
12. My senior management team doesn't understand the value of media work: see pages 105-107
13. I don't feel like our social media backs up our media work: see pages 96-99
14. I don't know what makes a good news story: see pages 34-52
15. We lack a comprehensive media strategy: read all of the book, but for a summary see pages 7-9
16. We work in a sensitive area so it's not easy to provide images or quotes: see pages 36-37.

USEFUL RESOURCES

CharityComms

CharityComms is the membership network for communications professionals working in UK charities. It aims to raise the standards of communications across the sector, to fly the flag for communications as a vital strategic function at the heart of charities, and to connect communications professionals through sharing best practice.

CharityComms offers a whole range of free best practice guides related to media relations, including

- Crisis communications for charities
- Show and tell: portraying beneficiaries and service users
- Branding inside out: a Best Practice Guide to charity branding
- Harnessing the talent: working with celebrities
- Perfect Pitch: linking voice and values
- CharityComms guide to social media for charities

All are available to download from CharityComms' website, where you can also find information on the benefits of joining the network: www.charitycomms.org.uk.

CharityComms also runs AskCharity, the free service linking journalists and charities. Journalists use it to find case studies, spokespeople and information from a wide range of charities. Charities use it to build their media contacts and coverage. Charities can register for free at www.charitycomms.org.uk/askcharity.

Fifth Estate

Fifth Estate is the Chartered Institute of Public Relations's not-for-profit group that supports CIPR members working with PR and communications in the not-for-profit sector. The CIPR is the professional body for public relations practitioners in the UK. www.cipr.co.uk

Justgiving

Justgiving offers a helpful blog that can help charities understand more about social media and how to create shareable content. blog.justgiving.com

Knowhow Nonprofit

This website provides a source of knowledge and e-learning for charities, social enterprises and community groups, including on PR, communications and social media. knowhownonprofit.org

Media.info

This offers a comprehensive list of all the UK's media titles. media.info/uk

Media Trust

The Media Trust works with the media industry to empower charities and communities to have a voice and be heard. www.mediatrust.org

Slack Communications

The Slack Communications website contains a useful resources section, which contains a large number of blogs and articles on topics such as PR tips, writing skills, and social media techniques. Its team also delivers consultancy and training on all areas of communications including media outreach, key messaging and social media.

Specialist press

- *Civil Society Media* (www.civilsociety.co.uk)
- *Third Sector* (www.thirdsector.co.uk)
- *Charity Times* (www.charitytimes.com)
- *Guardian* Voluntary Sector Network and *UK Fundraising* (www.theguardian.com/voluntary-sector-network) (www.fundraising.co.uk) often run useful articles on media and communications for charities, as well as on risk and wider charity sector issues.
- *PR Week* (www.prweek.com/uk) is a trade magazine for PRs and can provide useful insight into key sector trends and developments.
- *Press Gazette* (www.pressgazette.co.uk) is the trade magazine for journalists and provides a useful insight into the world of journalism and the press.

ABOUT THE AUTHOR

Becky Slack has worked for almost 20 years within media, including within television and radio production, print and online B2B and B2C journalism, fundraising, communications and events.

Just over a decade has been spent in and around the charity sector. She has been deputy editor of *Charity Times* magazine, editor of *Professional Fundraising* and publishing editor of *Charity Insight*, and has been a senior fundraiser for the British Red Cross, where she worked across corporate and major donors. In addition, she is a trustee of the Flying Seagull Project, a charitable arts and theatre company that uses play and laughter to improve the lives of sick and disadvantaged children around the world.

Her company, Slack Communications, provides PR and communications advice, support and skills to a range of clients, many of which are charitable organisations. Projects range from writing and implementing on-going national and international PR strategies, to conducting communications audits, to delivering special one-off profile-raising activities, such as rebrands, report launches or events.

In addition, her team writes and edits reports, special supplements and articles for government ministers, membership groups and national publishers on topics as diverse as poverty, housing, food security, investment strategies, political reform and everything else in between. They also deliver regular training sessions on topics such as marketing and communications, working with the media, enewsletters and content strategy.

Becky blogs for publications such as *Spears Wealth Management*, *UK Fundraising* and the Slack Communication's own website, and chairs political discussions and debates for the *New Statesman*. She is also an active member of the Women's Equality Party.

When she's not running Slack Communications, Becky loves to cook, travel, hang out with friends and family and, if there is any time left over, she's been known to write the occasional storybook for her friend's children.

For more information, visit www.slackcommunications.co.uk

INDEX

The Charity First Series

For the full list of titles in the Charity First Series, see www.charityfirstseries.org.

Titles already published include:
Academy Schools – from Conversion to Successful Operation
Beyond the Collection Plate - Developing Church Income from Different Sources
Data Protection for Fundraisers
Fundraising for Small Charities
Legacy Fundraising from Scratch
Major Gift Fundraising
Organising and Operating a US Charity
Prospect Research
Raising Funds from Grant Makers
Structuring Not-for-Profit Operations in the UK
The Gift Aid Guide

Also published by Social Partnership Marketing
Invisible Grantmakers - an annual listing of unpublished grantmaking trusts.
See www.socialpartnershipmarketing.co.uk for further details.